Patterns of Conventional Warfighting under the Nuclear Umbrella

Igor Davidzon

Patterns of Conventional Warfighting under the Nuclear Umbrella

palgrave
macmillan

Igor Davidzon
IR & Security Policy
Freie Universität Berlin
Berlin, Germany

ISBN 978-3-030-45596-5   ISBN 978-3-030-45594-1   (eBook)
https://doi.org/10.1007/978-3-030-45594-1

This Palgrave Pivot imprint is published by the registered company Springer Nature
Switzerland AG
The registered company address is: Gewerbestrasse 11, 6330 Cham, Switzerland

To Linda and Nadia

ACKNOWLEDGMENTS

This book was written by myself and I am solely responsible for its contents and conclusions. It should be noted that the Ph.D. research conducted by me paved the way for writing this book.

I would like to express my gratitude to my Ph.D. supervisor, Dr. Eitan Barak, for his support and advice during my Ph.D. research at the Hebrew University in Jerusalem.

As part of my postdoctoral studies at the Freie Universität in Berlin, I got to know and work collaboratively with Prof. Thomas Risse and Dr. Ingo Peters. The knowledge that I gained from them in the field of an academic research also substantially contributed to the writing of the book.

Special thanks goes to Avishai Sabag for his significant help in consolidating the economic data implemented in the study.

Finally, I would also like to thank my wife Nadia who has supported me all the way through the writing process until the publication of the book.

CONTENTS

ABOUT THE AUTHOR

Dr. Igor Davidzon is a Postdoctoral Research Fellow at Freie Universität Berlin Center for Transnational Relations, Foreign and Security Policy. He has a Ph.D. from the International Relations Department at Hebrew University in Jerusalem.

LIST OF FIGURES

CHAPTER 1

Introduction

Abstract How does nuclear weaponization affect the conventional warfighting patterns of the countries? Such a question becomes more relevant given the fact that following the detonation of two nuclear bombs by the United States (US) in August 1945 and conduction of tests by other first nuclear proliferation wave countries, few more countries which belong to the second nuclear proliferation wave acquired their nuclear weapon in the process of secret nuclear weaponization proliferation. The nuclear weaponization influenced the relations among the countries. The ultimate goal of this book is to examine the impact of nuclear weaponization on the warfighting patterns in respect of conventional conflicts openly waged by one state over another by regular armies. In order to address the aforementioned question, we examine the case studies of three countries, attributable to the second nuclear proliferation wave, which are not parties to NPT—Pakistan, India, and Israel.

Keywords Cold War · Neoclassical realism · Non-Proliferation Treaty · Nuclear weaponization · Patterns of warfighting

How does nuclear weaponization affect the conventional warfighting patterns of the countries? Such a question becomes more relevant given the fact that following the detonation of two nuclear bombs by the United States (US) in August 1945 and conduction of tests by other first

© The Author(s) 2020
I. Davidzon, *Patterns of Conventional Warfighting under the Nuclear Umbrella*,
https://doi.org/10.1007/978-3-030-45594-1_1

1

nuclear proliferation wave countries, few more countries which belong to the second nuclear proliferation wave acquired their nuclear weapon in the process of secret nuclear weaponization proliferation. The nuclear weaponization influenced the relations among the countries. The ultimate goal of this book is to examine the impact of nuclear weaponization on the warfighting patterns in respect of conventional conflicts openly waged by one state over another by regular armies.[1] In order to address the aforementioned question, we examine the case studies of three countries, attributable to the second nuclear proliferation wave, which are not parties to NPT—Pakistan, India, and Israel.[2] Our analysis appears to defer from the existing studies, inter alia, in view of the fact, that in contrast to other existing studies regarding the effects of nuclear weapons on conventional war possibility, we focus on conventional warfighting patterns in practice and argue that the nuclear weaponization influence is variable and after crossing the nuclear weaponization threshold various countries have adopted different approaches regarding the conventional warfighting patterns under the nuclear umbrella.

It should be noted that beyond the book's further contribution to scholarly literature on nuclear weapons, the importance of examining the impact of nuclear weaponization on warfighting patterns is particularly high even nowadays given the Iranian or, in the future, other countries' attempts to develop nuclear arsenal secretly and thus undermine

---

[1] Martin van Creveld (2004). *Modern Conventional Warfare: An Overview*, US. National Intelligence Council Workshop. http://www.offnews.info/downloads/2020modern_warfare.pdf. Accessed 18 June 2019.

[2] It should be noted that several case studies, associated with the second proliferation wave, were excluded from this study. North Korea has been excluded from this study due to its character as a totalitarian, isolated, and closed state with severe restrictions on freedom of information. The limited number of publications concerning its nuclear program, in addition to the fact that the majority of such publications rely on a single source—South Korean Intelligence—which is clearly biased by interests, appears not to allow the establishment of a factual basis for conducting research on security issues. As for South Africa, the nuclear roll-back that this country carried out in the early 1990s meant that the state possessed nuclear weapons for a relatively limited time (as of the early 1980s), a fact that does not allow for proper assessment of the effects of weaponization. In addition, although Ukraine, Belarus, and Kazakhstan remained after the collapse of the Soviet Union nuclear arsenal, these countries cannot be included in the group of case studies because they have not developed or even sought to develop nuclear weapons but rather "inherited" them in their territory after the collapse of the Soviet Union. Shortly after the collapse of the USSR, they handed over the nuclear arsenal to Russia.

NPT regime. Would it change their warfighting preferences? Would they adopt escalation and aggressive warfighting pattern at the battlefield or would they adopt restraint and defensive pattern?

Notwithstanding the fact that the literature on the NPT's five nuclear weapons states is abundant, mainly in respect of the so-called "balance of terror" in the Cold War era,[3] the experience of such countries, doesn't appear to be applicable for the purposes of examination of the nuclear weaponization influence on the warfighting patterns of the countries in the aforementioned three case studies.

As noted, compared to the first nuclear proliferation wave countries, which should be deemed to be nuclear pursuant to the Non-Proliferation Treaty (NPT),[4] the main characteristic of the second nuclear proliferation wave countries is that they secretly crossed the nuclear weaponization threshold even prior to performance of public nuclear tests and the process was incompatible with the NPT regime rules. The weaponization can be defined as follows:

> ...assembling nuclear weapons, i.e., fashioning weapon-grade fissile materials (plutonium or highly enriched uranium) into a bomb, by using a workable bomb design.[5]

Thus, the first wave countries demonstrate a different model regarding the process of nuclear weapon acquisition and the challenges that they had to face. In contrast to such countries, which obtained the nuclear weapon in course of the public tests, Pakistan and India secretly crossed the nuclear weaponization threshold even prior to performance of the public nuclear tests in 1998. In the Israeli case, no public test has been conducted up until the date hereof. Moreover, there has been no explicit acknowledgment by officials of the existence of a nuclear arsenal.

---

[3] See for example: Albert Wohlstetter (January 1959). The Delicate Balance of Power, *Foreign Affairs*, 37/2, 211–234; Alexander George & Richard Smoke (1974). *Deterrence in American Foreign Policy*, New York: Columbia University Press; Robert Jervis & Robert Ned Lebow (1985). *Psychology and Deterrence*, Baltimore: John Hopkins University Press; Lawrence Freedman (2003). *The Evolution of Nuclear Strategy*, New York: Palgrave Macmillan.

[4] This group of countries includes: the Soviet Union (1949), the Great Britain (1952), France (1960) and the Communist China (1964).

[5] David Albright & Mark Hibbs (1992). Pakistan's Bomb: Out of the Closet, *Bulletin of the Atomic Scientists*, 48/6 (39), 7.

As John Weltman argued, at the time, due to the technical progress, a country could possess a usable nuclear weapon without a need first to test it.[6]

It seems that a model of public introduction of nuclear weapon into a conflict, mainly, by two rival superpowers during the Cold War, Soviet Union and the United States, couldn't constitute a solid basis for examination of the impact of secret nuclear weaponization on countries' warfighting patterns.

Upon commencement of the nuclear weapon possession, the size and disposition of nuclear arsenal are vague from the other side's perspective.[7] Since acquiring nuclear capability could affect both belligerents' perceptions of relative power, public and acknowledged military nuclear capability is not associated with the same degree of uncertainty regarding adversary's actual nuclear status.

This nuclear condition is characterized by a high degree of confidentiality and is referred to in the academic literature as "Opacity":

> ... a situation in which a state's nuclear capability has not been acknowledged, but is recognized in a way that influences other nations' perceptions and actions.[8]

At a later stage, such a term was further developed. Thus, David Hagerty defined the concept as follows:

> Opaque proliferation is a government's covert development of nuclear weapon capabilities combined with its public denial of any intention to deploy nuclear weapons.[9]

---

[6] John Weltman (Winter 1981/1982). Managing Nuclear Multipolarity, *International Security*, 6/3, 183.

[7] Michal Krepon (2003). The Stability-Instability Paradox, Misperception, and Escalation Control in South Asia, Asia Dialogue, https://theasiadialogue.com/wp-content/uploads/2017/10/stability-instability-paradox-south-asia.pdf. Accessed 20 June 2019.

[8] https://theasiadialogue.com/wp-content/uploads/2017/10/stability-instability-paradox-south-asia.pdf.

Avner Cohen & Benjamin Frankel (1991). Opaque Nuclear Proliferation, in Frankel (Ed.), *Opaque Nuclear Proliferation: Methodological and Policy Implications* (pp. 14–41), London: Frank Press.

[9] Devin Hagerty (1998). *The Consequences of Nuclear Proliferation*, Cambridge: The MIT Press, 40.

Furthermore, as aforementioned, while previous studies focused mainly on the impact of nuclear weapons on deterrence, strategic stability,[10] namely, the subject of weaponization influence on warfighting at the conventional level, seems to be relatively neglected by scholars.

Moreover, nuclear deterrence's logic appears to be different. The aim of deterrence is to prevent a war. Nevertheless, by examining weaponization influence on warfighting, one is not interested to explore whether and how weaponization encourages deterrence but whether and to what extent it affects the traditional patterns of warfighting. Therefore, these theories cannot answer questions such as: Why does crossing a weaponization threshold affect differently warfighting patterns of Pakistan, India, and Israel? What is the causal mechanism of such influence? How do countries prefer one warfighting pattern over another? How do such choices affect conflicts?

Since the existing studies do not provide comprehensive answers to such important questions and rather focus on nuclear weapons influence on deterrence and conflicts stability than on its influence on conventional warfighting patterns, this book contributes to the research by broadening the scholarly discussion beyond and shift the focus from the study of nuclear weapons influence on deterrence to the examination of nuclear weaponization influence on countries' practical behavior in wars.

Accordingly, as will be discussed in detail below, we will examine the presumed variable influence of nuclear weaponization through the implementation of an alternative model, which is inspired by the neoclassical realism and consists of two concepts: the concept of a strategic threat and the concept of strategic culture. Such combined approach, focusing on external and internal variables, allows to examine differences in warfighting patterns the countries adopt as a result of nuclear weaponization and thus avoiding determinism that characterizes theories examining the effect of nuclear weapons on strategic stability.

---

[10]Regarding second nuclear proliferation countries see for example: Feroz Hassan Khan (Spring 2003). Challenges to Nuclear Stability in South Asia, *The Nonproliferation Review*, 10/1, 59–74; Amir Latif (June 2014). A Comparative Study of Nuclear Doctrines of India and Pakistan, *Journal of Global Peace and Conflict*, 2/1, 129–146; Michael Krepon, et al. (2015). *Deterrence Instability and Nuclear Weapons in South Asia*, Washington, DC: Stimson Center; Gurmeet Kanwal (2017). *Strategic Stability in South Asia: An India's Perspective*, Albuquerque: Sandia National Laboratories; Yair Evron (1994). *Israel's Nuclear Dilemma*, London: Routledge; Shai Feldman (1983). *Israeli Nuclear Deterrence*, Tel Aviv: HaKibbutz HaMeuchad.

Since there is no "one-size-fits-all" model to examine warfighting patterns under the nuclear umbrella, we identify and classify three models of nuclear weaponization influence:

- *Restraint Imposition*—referring to the situation in which a country, given a nuclear aggressive foe, is restrained and cannot activate its traditional pattern of warfighting.
- *Aggression Encouragement*—refers to the situation in which a weaker aggressive and revisionist country due to nuclear weaponization manages to maintain its traditional pattern of war management against a much stronger enemy.
- *Nuclear "Ignorance"*—refers to the situation in which a country, even a weaker one in relation to the enemy, doesn't rely on its nuclear arsenal and adopts warfighting patterns while ignoring a nuclear capability.

The focus on practical expression of military doctrines (i.e., warfighting patterns) derives from the fact that the examination of doctrines cannot necessarily facilitate detection of the nuclear weapons' impact. Warfighting patterns constitute a practical expression of military doctrines and reflect a country's military behavior in a war. The leaders of the countries tend to refrain from publicly stating how they will behave in a conventional war in view of nuclear weapons, even more so that they are reluctant to act in a certain manner as a result of the enemy nuclear deterrence. As Scott Sagan noted:

> ...there are strong internal and external reasons why senior government leaders might not want to spell out in advance, in public or even in classified documents, the details when or how they intend to use military force...[11]

Therefore, studying the actual combat of armies at the battlefield may provide reliable findings in this respect.

---

[11] Scott Sagan (2009). The Evolution of Pakistani and Indian Nuclear Doctrine, in S. Sagan (Ed.), *Inside Nuclear South Asia* (pp. 219–254), Stanford: Stanford University Press.

THE BOOK'S STRUCTURE

The first part of the book elaborates the models of influence of nuclear weaponization on patterns of conventional warfighting: *Aggression Encouragement, Restraint Imposition* and "*Nuclear Ignorance*". In order to explore the impact of nuclear weaponization, we review in Chapter 2 the existing literature regarding the nuclear weapons' impact on deterrence and strategic stability and present the theoretical framework of our analysis. In Chapter 3, we operationalize the external variable of strategic threat and internal one of strategic culture. Then, we identify and classify the three models of nuclear weaponization. Based on the theoretical framework, we argue that these models are the result of interpretation of change in distribution of relative power via the strategic culture variable by decision-makers.

The following three chapters are devoted to an empirical analysis. In Chapter 4, I briefly review the material components of relative power of the three examined case studies and proceed with the review of the strategic cultures as lens of decision-makers in Islamabad, Tel Aviv, and New Delhi for perception and interpretation of an objective reality of either power inferiority or superiority *vis-à-vis* rival country. On the basis of the perceptions, I elaborate the countries' patterns of warfighting before the weaponization era. Afterwards, I attribute each examined country to a specific model of a nuclear weaponization influence. In Chapter 5, I briefly review the history of nuclear development of Pakistan, India, and Israel. I identify herein the time period in which each of the case studies crossed the nuclear weaponization threshold. This identification is necessary in order to chronologically determine which conventional wars, fought by the three countries, occurred either in pre- or post-weaponization periods. Additionally, I argue that the nuclear programs aiming to produce a weapon was a result of traumatic events in the history of the countries: while in the Israeli case the decision to go nuclear was influenced by the events of the Holocaust, in the Pakistani and Indian cases it was the defeat in the war with India in 1971 and Pakistani nuclear threat, respectively, that caused to seek a nuclear weapon as a security assurance. In Chapter 6, I review the patterns of warfighting of the examined case studies in course of the two following periods, before and after crossing the weaponization threshold, as expressed during the conventional wars fought by the countries.

Based on the three models of nuclear weaponization influence, I explore the military patterns of Pakistani, Israeli, and Indian armies during the following wars: Sinai campaign (1956),[12] the Six-Day War (1967), Yom Kippur war (1973) regarding the Israeli case study; first Indo-Pak war (1947), second Indo-Pak war (1965), third Indo-Pak war (1971), and Kargil war (1999) regarding the Pakistani and Indian case studies.

It should be noted that the discussion regarding the Israeli case study excludes two wars which belong chronologically to the post-nuclear weaponization period—the War of Attrition (1969–1970) and the First Lebanon war (1982). The War of Attrition is substantially different from other wars (e.g., the Yom Kippur war and the Six-Day War), which were strategically conducted for the purpose of military decision. On the contrary in the absence of such characteristics, the aforementioned war should not be included in this research. As for the 1982 Lebanon War, I do not disregard the fact that during the war there were battles between the regular forces, the Israelis and the Syrians. However, the main focus of the war was sub-conventional fighting against the Palestinian "Fatah." In light of the above, in order not to distort the findings of the study, I excluded the case of this war from the discussion.

Additionally, due to the history of mutual hostility between India and Pakistan, the discussion regarding these two countries will be united into one subsection. Chapter 7 will be devoted to the summary of the discussion and conclusions.

[12] The Independence war, which broke out upon the establishment of the state in 1948, is not included in this study, due to the fact that during this war the Israeli army was established and its Israeli military doctrine was largely consolidated in light of the lessons learned based on the war and its consequences.

REFERENCES

Albright, D. & Hibbs, M. (1992). Pakistan's Bomb: Out of the Closet. *Bulletin of the Atomic Scientists*, 48/6 (39), 6–8.

Cohen, A. & Frankel, B. (1991). Opaque Nuclear Proliferation. In Benjamin Frankel (Ed.), *Opaque Nuclear Proliferation: Methodological and Policy Implications* (pp. 14–41). London: Frank Press.

Evron, Y. (1994). *Israel's Nuclear Dilemma*. London: Routledge.

Feldman, S. (1983). *Israeli Nuclear Deterrence*. Tel Aviv: HaKibbutz HaMeuchad.

Freedman, L. (2003). *The Evolution of Nuclear Strategy*. New York: Palgrave Macmillan.

George, A. & Smoke, R. (1974). *Deterrence in American Foreign Policy*. New York: Columbia University Press.

Hagerty, D. (1998). *The Consequences of Nuclear Proliferation*. Cambridge: The MIT Press.

Jervis, R. & Lebow, R. N. (1985). *Psychology and Deterrence*. Baltimore: John Hopkins University Press.

Kanwal, G. (2017). *Strategic Stability in South Asia: An India's Perspective*. Albuquerque: Sandia National Laboratories.

Khan, F. H. (Spring 2003). Challenges to Nuclear Stability in South Asia. *The Nonproliferation Review*, 10/1, 59–74.

Krepon, M. (2003). The Stability-Instability Paradox, Misperception, and Escalation Control in South Asia. Asia Dialogue. https://theasiadialogue. com/wp-content/uploads/2017/10/stability-instability-paradox-south-asia. pdf. Accessed 20 June 2019.

Krepon, M., et al. (2015). *Deterrence Instability and Nuclear Weapons in South Asia*. Washington, DC: Stimson Center.

Latif, A. (June 2014). A Comparative Study of Nuclear Doctrines of India and Pakistan. *Journal of Global Peace and Conflict*, 2/1, 129–146.

Sagan, S. (2009). The Evolution of Pakistani and Indian Nuclear Doctrine. In S. Sagan (Ed.), *Inside Nuclear South Asia* (pp. 219–254). Stanford: Stanford University Press.

van Creveld, M. (2004). *Modern Conventional Warfare: An Overview*. US. National Intelligence Council Workshop. http://www.offnews.info/down-loads/2020modern_warfare.pdf. Accessed 18 June 2019.

Weltman, J. (Winter 1981/1982). Managing Nuclear Multipolarity. *International Security*, 6/3, 182–194.

Wohlstetter, A. (January 1959). The Delicate Balance of Power. *Foreign Affairs*, 37/2, 211–234.

CHAPTER 2

Nuclear Weaponization and Warfighting Patterns—Theoretical Discussion

Abstract What is the impact of strategic culture perceptions on countries' military conduct? What are the findings of previous researches? To address such questions, we start the discussion with the review of the existing literature regarding the influence of nuclear proliferation on countries' warfighting patterns. Afterwards, we present our research model for the examination of warfighting patterns of three case studies. To understand the impact of strategic culture on the military behavior of the countries, we conclude the chapter with a brief overview of the strategic culture concept.

Keywords Nuclear optimism · Nuclear pessimism · Stability–instability paradox · Preexisting strategic threat

What is the impact of strategic culture perceptions on countries' military conduct? What are the findings of previous researches? To address such questions, we start the discussion with the review of the existing literature regarding the influence of nuclear proliferation on countries' warfighting patterns. Afterwards, we present our research model for the examination of warfighting patterns of three case studies. To understand the impact of strategic culture on the military behavior of the countries, we conclude the chapter with a brief overview of the strategic culture concept.

© The Author(s) 2020   11
I. Davidzon, *Patterns of Conventional
Warfighting under the Nuclear Umbrella,*
https://doi.org/10.1007/978-3-030-45594-1_2

Scholarly Debate on Nuclear Proliferation Impact

Optimists/Pessimists Debate

How does nuclear weapon affect international relations? Does it promote a strategic stability and decrease the possibility of war or vice versa increase the chances of an armed conflict? The preoccupation with these questions constitutes, to a great extent, a significant part of the scholarly literature on nuclear proliferation in the Cold War period. As Bell and Miller noted: "Whether nuclear weapons spur or dampen conventional interstate conflict has long been debated."[1] Indeed, the literature is split on the issue of nuclear weapon influence on conflicts and war probability.[2] On the one hand, proliferation optimists argue that the spread of devastating nuclear weapons increases stability among nations and prevents wars.[3] On the other hand, proliferation pessimists argue that the proliferation of nuclear weapons in the world increases a possibility of crisis instability and accidental and preventive wars.[4]

[1] Mark Bell & Nicholas Miller (2015). Questioning the Effect of Nuclear Weapons on Conflict, *The Journal of Conflict Resolution*, 59/1, 76.

[2] Victor Asal & Kyle Beardsley (2007). Proliferation and International Crisis Behavior, *Journal of Peace Research*, 44/2, 139.

[3] See for instance: Kenneth Waltz (1981). The Spread of Nuclear Weapons: More May Better, *Adelphi Papers*, 171, London: International Institute for Strategic Studies; John Mearsheimer (Summer 1990). Back to the Future: Instability in Europe After the Cold War, *International Security*, 15/1, 5–56; Asal & Beardsley, Proliferation and International Crisis Behavior, John Lewis Gaddis (Spring 1986). The Long Peace: Elements of Stability in the Postwar International System, *International Security*, 10/4, 99–142; Bruce Bueno de Mesquita & William Riker (June 1982). An Assessment of the Merits of Selective Nuclear Proliferation, *The Journal of Conflict Resolution*, 26/2, 283–306; David Karl (Winter 1996–1997). Proliferation Pessimism and Emerging Nuclear Powers, *International Security*, 21/3, 87–119; Shai Feldman (1982). *Israeli Nuclear Deterrence: A Strategy for the 1980s*, New York: Columbia University Press; Dagobert Brito & Michael Intriligator (March 1996). Proliferation and the Probability of a War: A Cardinality Theorem, *The Journal of Conflict Resolution*, 40/1, 206–214; Martin van Creveld (1993). *Nuclear Proliferation and the Future of Conflict*, New York: Free Press.

[4] See for instance: Scott Sagan, (1993). *The Limits of Safety: Organizations, Accidents and Nuclear Weapons*, Princeton: Princeton University Press; Peter Feaver (1993). Proliferation Optimism and Theories of Nuclear Operations, *Security Studies*, 2/3–4, 159–191; Steven Miller (Summer 1993). The Case Against a Ukrainian Nuclear Deterrent, *Foreign Affairs*, 72/3, 67–80; Jeffrey Knopf (Autumn 2002). Recasting the Optimism/Realism Debate, *Security Studies*, 12/1, 41–96; Bradley Thayer (Spring 1994). The Risk of Nuclear Inadvertence: A Review Essay, *Security Studies*, 3/3, 428–493; Bruce Blair

The optimistic assumptions are based, primarily, on the rational view of nuclear deterrence.[5] According to Mearsheimer:

> Deterrence is most likely to hold when the costs and risks of going to war are obviously great. The more horrible the prospect of war, the less likely it is to occur...Thus nuclear weapons are a superb deterrent: they guarantee high costs, and are more useful for self-defense than for aggression.[6]

Nuclear weapons are regarded as perfect deterrence against aggression.[7] Pursuant to the rational logic of nuclear deterrence, the optimists believe that regardless of the internal, political conditions or political culture of the nuclear countries, nuclear weapons cause caution in decision-makers in nuclear-armed states.[8] Thus, according to Kenneth Waltz, nuclear weapons should encourage countries' restraint:

> ...the higher the stakes and the closer a country moves toward winning them, the more surely that country invites retaliation and risks its own destruction. States are not likely to run major risks for minor gains. War between nuclear states may escalate as the loser uses and larger and larger warheads. Fearing that, states will want to draw back. Not escalation but de-escalation becomes more likely.[9]

Therefore, upon acquisition of nuclear weapons, adversaries become more cautious in their relations with each other.[10] Given the risk of a

(1993). *The Logic of Accidental War*, Washington, DC: Brookings; Lewis Dunn (1991). Containing Nuclear Proliferation, *Adelphi Paper*, 263, London: International Institute for Strategic Studies; Steven David (Winter 1992–1993). Why the Third World Still Matters, *International Security*, 17/3, 127–159.

[5] Asal & Beardsley, Proliferation and International Crisis Behavior, 143.

[6] Mearsheimer, Back to the Future, 19–20.

[7] John Mearsheimer (2000, March 23). India Needs the Bomb, *The New York Times*, https://www.nytimes.com/2000/03/24/opinion/india-needs-the-bomb.html. Accessed 16 February 2020.

[8] Peter Lavoy (1995). The Strategic Consequences of Nuclear Proliferation: A Review Essay, *Security Studies*, 4/4, 706.

[9] Scott Sagan & Kenneth Waltz (2003). *The Spread of Nuclear Weapons: A Debate Renewed*, New York: W. W. Norton, 6.

[10] Waltz (1981). *The Spread of Nuclear Weapons*, 9.

nuclear escalation, nuclear countries should exercise caution and not start a conventional war. Even authoritarian regimes with aggressive rhetoric toward other countries, became more cautious and restrained, due to their sensitivity to the costs associated with the nuclear weapons threat.[11] In this sense a nuclear weapon has a stabilizing effect and discourages an escalation process among adversaries, which otherwise could lead to a war threat.[12] Accordingly, given the high costs that a conflict's initiator would have to incur, the more nuclear-armed nations are beneficial for stability and prevention of escalation into a conventional conflict. Increasing the number of nuclear-armed states also contribute to a conflict's initiator uncertainty regarding other nuclear-armed countries reaction in the course of hostilities.[13] Similarly, Weltman, referring to nuclearization of regional conflicts, stated that given sufficient time, mutual deterrence dynamic between two nuclear rivals will be developed. Under these circumstances no rival, unconfident of its capability to destroy his enemy's nuclear arsenal, would take a risk associated with initiating a conflict.[14]

According to such logic (which is derived from the Cold War experience), however, referring to the situation in which state A and state B possess nuclear arsenal, optimists put greater emphasis on state B's considerations and pay less attention to state A's perception of its nuclear weapon role. The optimist approach ignores the situation that a nuclear state may perceive its nuclear arsenal as a change in relative power *vis-à-vis* a nuclear opponent and initiate a conventional war against him. In this sense, nuclear weapons would be regarded by state A as a shield against the adversary's reaction.

Hence, the nuclear optimists assumed that the new nuclear-armed powers should behave according to the same nuclear deterrence logic, as

[11] Sagan & Waltz (2003). *The Spread of Nuclear Weapons*, 14.

[12] Gaddis, The Long Peace, 123.

[13] Brito & Intriligator (March 1996). Proliferation and the Probability of a War, 208.

[14] Weltman, Managing Nuclear Multipolarity, 190. There are also approaches which support the optimistic assumptions by reference to domestic factors. In this respect, for instance, Maria Roust Rublee, addressing the question of nuclear restraint, referred to a social mechanism, an international social environment of non-proliferation movement, which influences states vision of a nuclear weapon and contributes to a nuclear restraint. See Maria Rost Rublee (2009). *Nonproliferation Norms: Why States Choose Nuclear Restrain*, Athens and London: University of Georgia Press.

it was during the Cold War between the two superpowers.[15] Thus, after the nuclear tests in 1998, there was room for hope in India that the declaration of nuclear capability would reduce Pakistani concerns regarding strategic asymmetry in favor of India.[16] Nevertheless, it seems that the history of Indo-Pakistani conflict contradicts this optimistic assumption. Despite the potential of escalation into nuclear conflict, both the countries waged a conventional war against each other in Kargil in 1999 even after crossing the weaponization threshold. As former chief of the Indian Army during Kargil war, General Ved Prakash Malik stated:

> [Al]though India and Pakistan are nuclear nations, it is not true to say there cannot be a conventional war between them. Kargil proved that.[17]

As abovementioned, the optimistic assumptions were challenged by the school of thought of nuclear pessimism. The pessimists, labeled by Lavoy as *conditional proliferation pessimists*, don't negate the optimistic fundamental assumptions based on rational deterrence logic but are concerned, that in contrast to two superpowers, other nuclear states may not proceed with the same rational deterrence logic and fail to take appropriate measures to prevent escalation, accidental or preventive war.[18] Despite Waltz's critic of Westerners approach adopted thereby *vis-à-vis* the people of Third World countries "in the old imperialistic manner," as "lesser breeds without the law",[19] nuclear pessimists argue that nuclear deterrence may not be stable in other regions.[20] For instance, David, referring to the possibility of nuclear weaponization among Third World states noted:

[15] Karl, Proliferation Pessimism and Emerging Nuclear Powers, 90.

[16] V. R. Raghavan (Fall/Winter 2001). Limited War and Nuclear Escalation in South Asia, *The Nonproliferation Review*, 2.

[17] The Rediff Interview with General Ved Prakash Malik, Part 3 (2001, July 28). Kargil Was a Good Wake-up Call, Rediff.com, https://m.rediff.com/news/2001/jul/28inter.htm. Accessed 20 June 2019.

[18] Lavoy, The Strategic Consequences of Nuclear Proliferation, 709.

[19] Sagan & Waltz, *The Spread of Nuclear Weapons*, 14.

[20] Scott Sagan (Spring 1994). The Perils of Proliferation: Organization Theory, Deterrence Theory and the Spread of Nuclear Weapons, *International Security*, 18/4, 67.

The intensity of the conflict faced by many Third World states also makes nuclear war more likely than among the great powers. It is true that the United States and the Soviet Union have had tense relations… Nevertheless, these countries have never experienced the degree of hostility that characterizes many Third World countries. Moreover, because the very existence of some Third World states is threatened, their resort to nuclear weapons becomes all the more probable.[21]

According to pessimists, assuming that each nuclear-armed state would adopt the same logic of rational nuclear deterrent, optimists pay less attention to internal, political characteristics of countries. Deviation from such logic can occur, pursuant to the pessimists, inter alia, due to nuclear command and control system failures, decision-makers miscalculations, organizational-bureaucratic influence on decision-making process in the state, etc. Thus, Sagan draws attention to the possibility that some future nuclear-armed countries might have professional military organizations, which without a proper civilian control, may have propensity toward organizational behavior, which would result in a deterrence failure. Subsequently, a behavior of military organizations, with their parochial interests and inflexible routines, are likely to result in a deterrence failure, either deliberate or accidental war.[22] Accordingly:

First, military officers, because of self-selection into the profession and socialization afterwards, are more inclined than the rest of the population to see war as likely in the near term and inevitable in the long run. The professional focus of attention on warfare also makes military officers skeptical of non-military alternatives to war, whereas civilian leaders often place stronger hopes on diplomatic and economic methods of long-term conflict resolution.[23]

Sagan also raised concern that due to the "lack of financial and organizational resources to produce adequate mechanical safety devices," some new nuclear states may be more prone (than the superpowers) to

---

[21] David, Why the Third World Still Matters, 152.

[22] Sagan & Waltz, *The Spread of Nuclear Weapons*, 42.

[23] Sagan, The Perils of Proliferation, 75–76. See also: Sagan & Waltz, *The Spread of Nuclear Weapons*, Chapter 2.

dangerous nuclear accidents, which could provoke further catastrophic escalation.[24]

Knopf argued that nuclear deterrence may fail and wars among nuclear-armed countries may erupt due to decision-makers considerations. Countries leaders might believe that a war is inevitable, get false warning of nuclear attack, or lose control of military units that are putting pressure to attack and not obeying the instructions of the central political authority.[25] Thus, under these circumstances states may initiate a preventive war.

Nevertheless, despite the differences among nuclear optimists and pessimists, both approaches are not applicable to examine a nuclear weaponization influence on countries warfighting and focused, primarily, on the connection between nuclear proliferation and outcomes.[26] Even the pessimists, who raise the possibility of deterrence failure, do not extend the discussion beyond the influence of the nuclear weapons on conflict stability and probability of war. Since the optimism/pessimism debate was mainly devoted to the question whether nuclear proliferation increases or decreases a probability of wars,[27] the existing literature less stressed the issue of variability of countries warfighting patterns under the nuclear umbrella. Moreover, while discussing the impact of nuclear weapons on relations and stability among nuclear-armed countries, both approaches do not raise the possibility of attacking a nuclear state by a conventional-armed enemy, as it occurred in the Israeli case.

Stability/Instability Paradox

Another prominent approach, which assumed that a nuclear weapon has a more complicated and nuanced effect on different conflict's levels, is the stability–instability paradox.[28] The concept of the stability–instability paradox is ascribed to a 1965 essay of Glenn Snyder "The Balance of

---

[24] Sagan & Waltz, *The Spread of Nuclear Weapons*, 72.

[25] Knopf, Recasting the Optimism-Pessimism Debate, 59.

[26] Mark Bell (July 2015). Beyond Emboldenment: How Acquiring Nuclear Weapons Can Change Foreign Policy, *International Security*, 40/1, 89.

[27] Matthew Kroenig (November 2009). Beyond Optimism and Pessimism: The Differential Effects of Nuclear Proliferation, *Managing the Atom Working Paper 2009–14*, Harvard Kennedy School, 2.

[28] Bell & Miller, Questioning the Effect of Nuclear Weapons on Conflict, 76.

Power and the Balance of Terror." In this work the author stated as follows:

> The greater the stability of the strategic balance of terror, the lower the stability of the overall balance at its lower levels of violence. The reasoning is that if neither side has a "full first-strike capability," and both know it, they will be less inhibited about initiating conventional war, and about the limited use nuclear weapons, than if the strategic balance were unstable. Thus, firm stability in the strategic nuclear balance tends to destabilize the conventional balance...[29]

The term "strategic stability" emerged during the Cold War era and referred to mutual deterrence dynamic between the Soviets and the Americans. Its logic is derived from the assumption that neither side sees the first use of a nuclear weapon as an effective strategy against an enemy. Due to survivability of both countries' nuclear forces and command and control systems, striking first is not expected to grant any advantage.[30]

Accordingly, the nuclear arsenals of two superpowers, USSR and the United States, encouraged the violence at lower levels of conflict among the superpowers through the proxies (e.g., Vietnam, Afghanistan) by ensuring that both sides would not escalate into a nuclear, strategic level of confrontation.

The logic behind such a dynamic is that as the likelihood of use of nuclear weapon increases and the nuclear stability is decreased, the likelihood of a conventional conflict decreases and the conventional stability is expected to increase. On the other hand, as the likelihood of nuclear weapons use decreases and the nuclear stability increases, the likelihood of conventional conflict shall increase and the conventional stability is expected to be reduced.[31]

---

[29] Glenn Snyder (1965). The Balance of Power and the Balance of Terror, in Paul Seabury (Ed.), *The Balance of Power* (p. 197), Scranton: Chandler. See also Robert Jervis (1984). *The Illogic of American Nuclear Strategy*, Ithaca: Cornell University Press.

[30] Elbridge Colby (February 2013). Defining Strategic Stability: Reconciling Stability and Deterrence, in Elbridge Colby & Michael Gerson (Eds.), *Strategic Stability: Contending Interpretations* (p. 48), Carlisle Barracks, PA: Strategic Studies Institute and U.S. Army War College Press.

[31] Paul Kapur (October 2017). Stability-Instability Paradox, in *The SAGE Encyclopedia of Political Behavior*, Thousand Oaks: Sage, http://sk.sagepub.com/reference/the-sage-encyclopedia-of-political-behavior/i10665.xml. Accessed 19 June 2019.

This approach benefits from great popularity among scholars studying the nuclear situation in South Asia.[32] As stated, for instance, by Knopf:

> These flare-ups in South Asia since the Indian and Pakistani nuclear tests of 1998 indicate the continued relevance of Glenn Snyder's stability-instability paradox.[33]

Despite the popularity of the stability–instability concept, however, it has a number of flaws.

First, it suffers from a lack of consensus with regard to its mechanism.[34] The literature is unclear as to how precisely the paradox causes the instability in South Asia.[35] As Mario Carranza mentioned:

> The overuse of the stability/instability paradox in the post test literature on the Indo-Pakistani nuclear competition has converted the concept into an oxymoron; it means different things to different scholars who tend to freely paraphrase Snyder's original formulation.[36]

Some scholars emphasized the escalation mechanism of the paradox. Lavoy, for instance, argued that despite their hostile relations, neither Pakistan nor India is willing to assume a risk of a nuclear war in order to settle any of their disputes.[37] According to Paul Kapur, scholars, which

---

[32] Rajesh Rajagopalan (February 2006). What Is Stability-Instability Paradox? Substantial Conflicts and the Nuclear Risk in South Asia, *SASSU Research Paper*, 4, 3–12. See also: Lavoy, The Strategic Consequences of Nuclear Proliferation, 739–740; P. R. Chari (June 2001). Nuclear Restraint, Nuclear Risk Reduction and the Security-Insecurity Paradox in South Asia, in Michael Krepon & Chris Gagne (Eds.), *The Stability-Instability Paradox: Nuclear Weapons and Brinksmanship in South Asia*, Report 38 (11–35), Washington, DC: The Henry Stimson Center; Sumit Ganguly (2002). *Conflict Unending: India-Pakistan Tensions Since 1947*, New Delhi: Oxford University Press, 122–123; Sumit Ganguly & Harrison Wagner (September 2004). India and Pakistan: Bargaining in the Shadow of Nuclear War, *Journal of Strategic Studies*, 27/3, 479–507.

[33] Knopf, Recasting the Optimism-Pessimism Debate, 52.

[34] Cristopher Watterson (2017). Competing Interpretations of the Stability-Instability Paradox: The Case of the Kargil War, *The Nonproliferation Review*, 24/1–2, 84.

[35] Paul Kapur (Fall 2005). India and Pakistan's Unstable Peace: Why Nuclear Asia Is Not Like Cold War Europe, *International Security*, 30/2, 131.

[36] Mario Esteban Carranza (2009). *South Asian Security and International Nuclear Oder*, Farnham: Ashgate Publishing Limited, 80.

[37] Lavoy, The Strategic Consequences of Nuclear Proliferation, 739.

referred to the escalation causal model in South Asia, interpret the mechanism in one of the following ways: (a) the possibility of low-level conflict escalating into a nuclear war and thereby encourages violence in the region; (b) the lack of possibility of escalation up to the nuclear level allows low-level violence.[38]

On the other hand, Michael Cohen in his social–psychological research of stability–instability paradox in South Asia, argued that personal learning of the leaders from their own experience during previous crisis contributes to moderation of countries revisionism and violence.[39] The problem with this argument, however, is that it cannot explain the ongoing confrontation between Pakistan and India. If the leaders of Pakistan engage in personal learning of challenges and risks of nuclear confrontation, it would be expected that at some point they will not just moderate their aggression but strive to stop it, to avoid any possibility of nuclear escalation. The cumulative learning would gradually "convince" decision-makers in Pakistan regarding the dangerous possibility of escalation, the risk that even a limited conflict could potentially get out of control.

Second, beyond the lack of clarity of the paradox's causal mechanism, the Indo-Pakistani conflict lacks some essential characteristics of Soviet–American rivalry, as a model of stability–instability paradox. During the Cold War, the strategy stability, i.e., a low likelihood of nuclear escalation in Europe, encouraged aggressive stance of the Soviet Union at lower levels, as a revisionist player, because Soviet troops were conventionally stronger than NATO. These conditions, however, don't apply to India–Pakistani relations. Pakistan, despite its revisionist aggressive policy, is on conventional level substantially weaker than India. Pursuant to the rational logic of stability–instability paradox, a stable strategic nuclear environment, in which nuclear escalation is unlikely, should encourage a violence at the conventional level, in which, as aforementioned, Islamabad has a clear disadvantage in comparison to New Delhi. As Kapur argued:

---

[38] Kapur, India and Pakistan's Unstable Peace, 131.

[39] Michael Cohen (2013). How Nuclear South Asia Is Like Cold War Europe, *Nonproliferation Review*, 20/3 (13), 442.

If a high degree of strategic stability prevailed, Pakistan would face strong incentives to avoid aggressive behavior; a small possibility of subnuclear Indo-Pakistani conflict spiraling to the nuclear behavior would reduce the ability of Pakistani nuclear weapons to deter an Indian conventional attack.[40]

Pakistan adopted the first use policy regarding its nuclear weapon to deter India's possessing superior military capabilities. According to Feroz Hassan Khan, who was a Director Arms Control and Disarmament Affairs in the Pakistan's Strategic Plans Division, Pakistan would adopt no first use policy regarding its nuclear weapon, it would negate the vary rational to develop this weapon.[41] Since both rivals, India and Pakistan, affect each other's strategic policies, at both the nuclear and conventional level, the mutual understanding regarding the low likelihood of nuclear weapon use, would discredit the Islamabad's threats to use its nuclear arsenal in a crisis. In light of the foregoing, stability–instability paradox couldn't explain Pakistani aggressive behavior, especially since the introduction of nuclear dimension to the India–Pakistan conflict in the late 1980s. According to the former Pakistani Prime Minister Benazir Bhutto, interviewed by Kapur: "she and other Pakistani leaders concluded that having nuclear capability would ensure that India could not launch a conventional war, knowing that it if did, it would turn nuclear, and that hundreds of millions would die... It would have meant suicide not just for one, but for both nations." Consequently, in the late 1980s Pakistan began to provide assistance to the anti-Indian forces in Kashmir. Moreover, in contrast to superpowers example, Pakistan adopted a first use nuclear policy against a possibility of crossing its border by Indian forces in course of a conventional conflict.[42]

Similarly, we cannot explain by means of the the paradox's logic the Indian restraint during Kargil war in 1999. Before Kargil war, the Indian army tended to respond to Pakistani aggression by escalating a conflict and crossing the border and expanding the geographical scope of

[40] Kapur, India and Pakistan's Unstable Peace, 140–141.

[41] India-Pakistan Nuclear Escalation—Where Could It Lead (2019, August 29). *Nature*, https://www.nature.com/articles/d41586-019-02578-5. Accessed 2 September 2019.

[42] Vipin Narang (2014). *Nuclear Strategy in the Modern Era*, Princeton and Oxford: Princeton University Press, 76.

hostilities. Nevertheless, in Kargil war the Indians refrained to cross the Pakistani border.[43] It seems that had India been certain that the likelihood of escalation to a nuclear war is low, it is reasonable to assume that it would not have behaved with such unusual restraint. In that case, we could assume that New Delhi would not have hesitated to cross the border in order to resolve the conflict.

Third, and not less important, similarly to optimist and pessimist approaches, the stability–instability paradox refers to the situation in which two or more adversaries possess a nuclear weapon. It doesn't apply, however, to the case of Israel, which so far exclusively held nuclear weapons in the Middle East and faces enemies lacking such capabilities. For such reasons it cannot be applicable as an overall model to study the three cases of second proliferation wave's countries.

RESEARCH MODEL

In view of non-applicability of the existing theoretical approaches to examine the presumed influence of weaponization on conventional warfighting, we implement an alternative model, which is inspired by the neoclassical realism and based on two concepts: the concept of a strategic threat, consists of material power components and a concept of strategic culture. A combined approach, focusing on external and internal variables, appears to be an appropriate one for analysis of highly complicated questions such as nuclear weaponization and its variable influence on conventional war fighting. In contrast to the deterministic assumptions regarding the positive or negative impact of nuclear weapons on war likelihood, which are associated with optimists/pessimists debate, we argue that with regard to the conventional warfighting under the nuclear umbrella, due to the different relative power perceptions of the countries, which crossed a nuclear weaponization threshold, nuclear weaponization affects variably the countries' conduct at the battlefield. The nuclear weaponization influence on the countries' warfighting patterns may be reflected in one of the three models, which will be discussed in detail in the next chapter: *Restraint Imposition, Aggression Encouragement, Nuclear "Ignorance."*

---

[43]The Rediff Interview with General Ved Prakash Malik, Part 1, (2001, July 26). Crossing the LoC Would Have Hade Other Implications, Rediff.com, https://m.rediff.com/news/2001/jul/26inter.htm. Accessed 20 June 2019.

Furthermore, in contrast to the abovementioned theoretical approaches, we draw a distinction between two kinds of conflicts: (a) nuclear weapon possession by two adversaries and (b) nuclear weapon possession exclusively by one.

Accordingly, we classify conventional warfighting patterns along the continuum of *escalation* versus *restraint* and *defense* versus *offensive*. The relative material power considerations are the basis for adopting a specific way to fight a war. It forms a pre-existing strategic threat and refers to the essential components of relative material power of countries *vis-à-vis* its adversaries: geostrategic situation, size and quality of the armed forces and economic power, mainly, militaries' budgets. The external strategic threat, however, doesn't influence directly decision-makers' choices regarding warfighting patterns. Its influence is indirect through the strategic culture layer.

We use the definition of strategic culture based on the concept developed by Alastair Johnston. According to him, strategic culture comprises of two levels: symbolic and operational.[44] Since strategic culture forms a relative power perception, through which decision-makers assess the reality, we refer to the symbolic level as a set of beliefs and assumptions regarding the geostrategic environment, country's self-image, and the threat posed by an enemy. Such beliefs and assumptions provide to decision-makers the necessary information regarding a balance of power *vis-à-vis* other adversaries and thus reduces uncertainty. Based on the symbolic level, the second operational part refers to the assumptions associated with the efficiency of strategic options, i.e., the available patterns of warfighting. This operational level constitutes the chain of causation between cultural variable and military behavior.

Strategic culture evolves from strategic threats, which countries face, and is the prism through which decision-makers interpret strategic threats. As Janice Gross Stein argued, political leaders tend to simplify the complexities of reality. Their simplified definition of the problem limited solution options for consideration. This both pushed other options, incompatible with the simplified reality perception, off the table and restricted the decision-making process to restricted choices.[45]

---

[44] Alastair Iain Johnston (1995). *Cultural Realism: Strategic Culture and Grand Strategy in Chinese History*, Princeton, NJ: Princeton University Press, 37–38.

[45] Janice Gross Stein (2016). Foreign Policy Decision Making: Rational, Psychological and Neurological Models, in Steve Smith, Amelia Hadfield, & Tin Dunne (Eds.), *Foreign Policy: Theories, Actors, Cases* (p. 133), Oxford: Oxford University Press.

In this sense, strategic culture serves as a platform for simplifying reality. The tendency to ignore inconsistent information frequently causes the strengthening of beliefs and their persistence. Long-term belief in other's hostility is easy to confirm and difficult to disprove regardless of the objective reality.[46]

Decision-makers are socialized into strategic culture, which is rooted in the countries' historical events. Based on attitudes and beliefs regarding the strategic environment, their country and enemy (a threat posed by him), decision-makers chose among the options the preferred warfighting pattern. As Feroz Hasan Khan argued:

> [These] "beliefs" ... grew out of existential threats in a historical narrative that was internalized thorough generations and that forms the inherent cognitive disposition of the people.[47]

To put it simply, pre-existing strategic threat affects patterns of warfighting through intervening variable of subjective cultural perceptions of countries' decision-makers (on political and military levels), which "distorts" a choice of a country under rational predictions of stability–instability paradox.

In view of the foregoing, a threat, even a similar one, could be perceived differently by the countries due to the cultural variable. This doesn't mean that varying perception necessarily generates different patterns of warfighting. It is probable that different cultural self-images (e.g., the "siege mentality" in the Israeli case or two-nation theory and Kashmir narratives in the Pakistani one) could cause adoption of similar patterns.

The attitudes and beliefs at the symbolic level of strategic culture tend to persist, but in view of a change in a relative power perception, the preference of warfighting pattern deriving from the symbolic level could be either changed or preserved. Since the nuclear weaponization leads to a clear change in relative material power of the countries, we suggest that this change will influence, via the strategic culture prism, the patterns of warfighting. Crossing nuclear weaponization threshold can lead

---

[46] Gross Stein, Foreign Policy Decision Making, 134–135.

[47] Feroz Hassan Khan (2012). *Eating Grass: The Making of the Pakistani Bomb,* Stanford: Stanford University Press, 4.

to preservation of the existing pattern of warfighting or to a change in the pattern of warfighting and adoption of another one which is consistent with the strategic culture predispositions.

Subsequently, we distinguish between two situations in pre- and post-weaponization periods: a weak state and a strong state in terms of relative material power.

In the pre-weaponization period the weaker the state, that is a country with less relative material power, the greater the likelihood, that such country will prefer an offensive warfighting pattern with a tendency to escalate during crisis. The adoption of this pattern is derived from the perception of power inferiority *vis-à-vis* the uncompromising enemy, which possesses significant and even existential threat and/or revisionist beliefs resulting from a historic political–territorial dispute.

At the other end of the scale is a strong state in terms of relative intensity. The stronger a country the greater likelihood, that such a country will prefer a defensive, restrained warfighting pattern at least at the beginning of the conflict, with a tendency to escalate and act offensively after a start of hostilities. The adoption of this pattern is derived from the perception of power superiority *vis-à-vis* a weaker enemy, even an aggressive one, which didn't possess existential threat.

As the long-term beliefs regarding countries' national self-image, perception of enemy tends to persist, the weaponization influence could be predicted as follows:

In the interstate conflict, with the possession of a nuclear arsenal by both countries, a weaker state will be encouraged by nuclear weapon acquisition to persist with the existing pattern of offensive and escalating warfighting. On the other hand, the stronger state will still demonstrate restraint, but without tendency to escalate and act offensively in the course of a conflict, due to the perception of an aggressive, revisionist enemy, which is now equipped with the destructive power of a nuclear weapon.

In the interstate conflict, with the possession of a nuclear arsenal only by one weaker country, its nuclear weapon will not influence its traditional patterns of warfighting. Such ignorance will be due to the unchangeable relative power perception of a nuclear state.

Strategic Culture and Military Behavior

In this section in order to deepen our understanding of the strategic culture impact on the countries' military conduct, we briefly review the strategic culture concept and its supposed impact on countries' military behavior.

The cultural aspect began to pave the way in the field of political science in the 1960s and the theory of political culture has been a pioneer in the development of behavioral research.[48] Interest in political culture arose largely due to the tragic events that preceded the outbreak of the World War II and led to the fall of several democratic regimes in Europe, while others managed to survive as democracies.[49]

Nevertheless, the term strategic culture first came into use in the late 1970s: in 1977, Jack Snyder used the term for the first time to explain the differences in attitudes between the Americans and the Soviets regarding nuclear strategy. According to him:

> Strategic culture can be defined as the sum total of ideas, conditional emotional responses, and patterns of habitual behavior that members of a national strategic community have acquired through instruction or imitation and share with each other with regard to nuclear strategy.[50]

Snyder argued that the Soviet's different view of such issues like nuclear deterrence and escalation, is due to Moscow's unique strategic situation, historical legacy, and the role that the military has played in the political process. From such a point of view, changes in Soviet strategic thought won't happen directly as a response to a change in the strategic environment but mediated by preexisting cultural beliefs.[51]

Snyder's research paved the way for additional studies in the field of strategic culture, which also dealt with superpower relations during the

---

[48] Stephen Welch (1993). *The Concept of Political Culture*, London: The Macmillan Press, 3–4.

[49] Ronald Inglehart (1997). *Modernization and Postmodernization: Cultural, Economic and Political Change in 43 Societies*, Princeton, NJ: Princeton University Press, 171.

[50] Jack L. Snyder (1977). *The Soviet Strategic Culture: Implications for Limited Nuclear Operations*, Santa Monica: Rand, 8.

[51] Snyder, *The Soviet Strategic Culture*, 38.

Cold War.[52] Nevertheless, one of the main problems of these first studies was the determinism of a pattern of behavior.[53] Addressing differences in American and Soviet strategic thought, Snyder argued that "the notions of a uniquely Soviet crisis style and a uniquely Soviet approach to strategic thought are elements in a broader conception of a Soviet strategic culture."[54] In other words, a unique Soviet strategic culture generated a unique pattern of behavior and thought.

As I already mentioned, different cultural perceptions could lead, however, to the adoption of similar warfighting patterns. How do unique cultural perceptions result in similar behavior? In this case, the behavioral determinism doesn't provide for a causal mechanism to answer this question. Under the assumption that strategic culture necessarily leads to one type of behavior, the possibility of behavior patterns optionality is excluded. Countries with unique strategic cultures assess and choose among the available options of behavior the preferred one, which is "appropriate" in terms of culture. By referring to the strategic culture as a tool for interpretation and options assessment, one can explain why do two unique strategic cultures cause a similar warfighting pattern.

In the 1980s, further research expanded the concept of strategic culture, stating that there is not necessarily a direct link between the declarative strategic culture and behavior patterns.[55] In their view, strategic culture is an instrument used by the political elites. Bradley Klein referred to the concept of strategy culture from Gramscian perspective of hegemony.[56] For Antonio Gramsci, a hegemony is a political production of ruling-class dominance over subordinate classes. Such dominance is established not due to violence and coercion but rather by the instrumentalization of hegemonic ideas, called "dominant ideology."[57]

---

[52] See for example: Colin Gray (1986). *Nuclear Strategy and National Style*. Boston: Hamilton Press.

[53] Johnston, *Cultural Realism*, 20.

[54] Snyder, *The Soviet Strategic Culture*, 13.

[55] This research wave includes for example studies of: Robin Luckham (1984). The Armament Culture, *Alternatives*, 10, 1–44; Bradley Klein (April 1988). Hegemony and Strategic Culture: American Power Projection and Alliance Defense Politics, *Review of International Studies*, 133–148.

[56] Klein, Hegemony and Strategic Culture, 135.

[57] Stephen Gill & David Law (December 1989). Global Hegemony and the Structural Power of Capital, *International Studies Quarterly*, 33/4, 476.

Similarly, a declarative instrumentalized strategic culture serves not for prioritizing of available patterns of violence derived from beliefs and attitudes of decision-makers. It is a tool to legitimize the power of decision-makers' group within a country aiming to operational strategies, which doesn't necessarily reflect the declared intentions but interests of this elite group. Thus, according to Bradly, while the American declarative nuclear policy during the Cold War was explained in terms of defensiveness, retaliation, and deterrence, the operational policy, however, emphasized active counterforce warfighting.[58]

Pursuant to this approach one can identify a manipulative aspect of culture due to the fact that it allows leaders or a dominant elite group to use strategic culture as a means for achieving their goals. The problem is that the distinction between declarative culture legitimizing decision-makers' authority and behavior reflecting the interests of decision-makers necessarily creates a disconnection between the cultural variable and the behavior.[59] Thus, it is difficult to determine that specific attitudes caused a specific type of behavior.

After the end of the Cold War the new wave of researches appeared in the 1990s.[60] A significant contribution to this rediscovery of strategic culture theory can be attributed to the constructivism, which began to gain momentum in the study of international relations in the post-Cold War era.[61] This research wave avoided the determinism that characterized the early research on the subject, but presented, however, different approaches in formulating the concept of culture and its impact on countries' behavior.[62] Elizabeth Kier defines a culture as a "tool kit" proposing choices between either an offensive or defensive military doctrine which are best understood from a cultural perspective:

[58] Klein, Hegemony and Strategic Culture, 138.

[59] Johnston, Thinking About Strategic Culture, 40.

[60] Johnston, Thinking About Strategic Culture, 41. See also: Michael C. Desch (1998). Assessing the Importance of Ideas in Security Studies, *International Security*, 23, 148. This research wave includes for example studies of: Elizabeth Kier (Spring 1995). Culture and Military Doctrine: France Between the Wars, *International Security*, 65–93; Peter Katzenstein, (1996). *Cultural Norms and National Security: Police and Military in Postwar Japan*, Ithaca and London: Cornell University Press; Jeffrey W. Legro (1995), *Cooperation Under Fire*, Ithaca and London: Cornell University Press.

[61] Jeffrey S. Lantis (2002), Strategic Culture and National Security Policy, *International Security Review*, 4, 96.

[62] Johnston, Thinking About Strategic Culture, 41.

...culture contains certain approaches to a variety of issues that provide each military with a finite number of ways to order behavior.[63]

On the other hand, Jeffrey Legro refers to such a concept as a prism used to interpret events or information in an uncertain environment.[64] Therefore, the choice between escalation and restraint is derived from the strategic culture context.[65]

Our choice of approach to strategic culture concept elaborated by Johnston (which also belongs chronologically to third wave research) is motivated by the fact that since culture, either as a "tool kit" or as a prism, creates preference of the behavior pattern, then the ideational explanation of where this limited options come from is required.[66] Therefore, it's necessary to provide such explanation by addressing a symbolic level of strategic culture, which elaborate decision-makers' interpretation of reality as a source of a choice preference. Additionally, the restricted choices repertoire between polar option of either escalation versus restraint or defense versus offense ignores additional possibilities such as the combination of these optional patterns of behavior, as presented by the current research.

References

Asal, V. & Beardsley, K. (2007). Proliferation and International Crisis Behavior. *Journal of Peace Research*, 44/2, 139–155.

Bell, M. (July 2015). Beyond Emboldenment: How Acquiring Nuclear Weapons Can Change Foreign Policy. *International Security*, 40/1, 87–119.

Bell, M. & Miller, N. (2015). Questioning the Effect of Nuclear Weapons on Conflict. *Journal of Conflict Resolution*, 59/1, 74–92.

Blair, B. (1993). *The Logic of Accidental War*. Washington, DC: Brookings.

Carranza, M. E. (2009). *South Asian Security and International Nuclear Oder*. Farnham: Ashgate Publishing Limited.

Chari, P. R. (June 2001). Nuclear Restraint, Nuclear Risk Reduction and the Security-Insecurity Paradox in South Asia. In Michael Krepon & Chris Gagne (Eds.), *The Stability-Instability Paradox: Nuclear Weapons and Brinksmanship*

---

[63] Kier, Culture and Military Doctrine, 79.

[64] Legro, *Cooperation Under Fire*, 22.

[65] Legro, *Cooperation Under Fire*, 28.

[66] Johnston, Thinking About Strategic Culture, 42–43.

in South Asia. Report 38 (pp. 11–35). Washington, DC: The Henty Stimson Center.

Cohen, M. (2013). How Nuclear South Asia Is Like Cold War Europe. *Nonproliferation Review*, 20/3 (13), 433–451.

Colby, E. (February 2013). Defining Strategic Stability: Reconciling Stability and Deterrence. In Elbridge Colby & Michael Gerson (Eds.), *Strategic Stability: Contending Interpretations* (pp. 47–83). Carlisle Barracks, PA: Strategic Studies Institute and U.S. Army War College Press.

David, S. (Winter 1992–1993). Why the Third World Still Matters. *International Security*, 17/3, 127–159.

de Mesquita, B. B. & Riker, W. (June 1982). An Assessment of the Merits of Selective Nuclear Proliferation. *Journal of Conflict Resolution*, 26/2, 283–306.

Desch, M. C. (Summer 1998). Assessing the Importance of Ideas in Security Studies, *International Security*, 23, 141–170.

Dunn, L. (1991). Containing Nuclear Proliferation. *Adelphi Paper*, 263. London: International Institute for Strategic Studies.

Feaver, P. (1993). Proliferation Optimism and Theories of Nuclear Operations. *Security Studies*, 2/3–4, 159–191.

Feldman, S. (1982). *Israeli Nuclear Deterrence: A Strategy for the 1980s*. New York: Columbia University Press.

Gaddis, J. L. (Spring 1986). The Long Peace: Elements of Stability in the Postwar International System. *International Security*, 10/4, 99–142.

Ganguly, S. (2002). *Conflict Unending: India-Pakistan Tensions Since 1947*. New Delhi: Oxford University Press.

Ganguly, S. & Wagner, H. (September 2004). India and Pakistan: Bargaining in the Shadow of Nuclear War. *Journal of Strategic Studies*, 27/3, 479–507.

Gill, S. & Law, D. (December 1989). Global Hegemony and the Structural Power of Capital. *International Studies Quarterly*, 33/4, 475–499.

Gray, C. (1986). *Nuclear Strategy and National Style*. Boston: Hamilton Press.

Gross Stein, J. (2016). Foreign Policy Decision Making: Rational, Psychological and Neurological Models. In Steve Smith, Amelia Hadfield, & Tin Dunne (Eds.), *Foreign Policy: Theories, Actors, Cases* (pp. 130–146). Oxford: Oxford University Press.

Inglehart, R. (1997). *Modernization and Postmodernization: Cultural, Economic and Political Change in 43 Societies*. Princeton, NJ: Princeton University Press.

Jervis, R. (1984). *The Illogic of American Nuclear Strategy*. Ithaca: Cornell University Press.

Johnston, A. I. (1995). *Cultural Realism: Strategic Culture and Grand Strategy in Chinese History*. Princeton, NJ: Princeton University Press.

Johnston, A. I. (Spring 1995). Thinking About Strategic Culture. *International Security*, 19/4, 32–64.

Kapur, P. (Fall 2005). India and Pakistan's Unstable Peace: Why Nuclear Asia Is Not Like Cold War Europe. *International Security*, 30/2, 127–152.

Kapur, P. (October 2017). Stability-Instability Paradox. *The SAGE Encyclopedia of Political Behavior*. Thousand Oaks: Sage. http://sk.sagepub.com/reference/the-sage-encyclopedia-of-political-behavior/i10665.xml. Accessed 19 June 2019.

Karl, D. (Winter 1996–1997). Proliferation Pessimism and Emerging Nuclear Powers. *International Security*, 21/3, 87–119.

Katzenstein, P. (1996). *Cultural Norms and National Security: Police and Military in Postwar Japan*. Ithaca and London: Cornell University Press.

Khan, F. H. (2012). *Eating Grass: The Making of the Pakistani Bomb*. Stanford: Stanford University Press.

Kier, E. (Spring 1995). Culture and Military Doctrine: France Between the Wars. *International Security*, 65–93.

Klein, B. (April 1988). Hegemony and Strategic Culture: American Power Projection and Alliance Defense Politics. *Review of International Studies*, 133–148.

Knopf, J. (Autumn 2002). Recasting the Optimism-Pessimism Debate. *Security Studies*, 12/1, 41–96.

Kroenig, M. (November 2009). Beyond Optimism and Pessimism: The Differential Effects of Nuclear Proliferation. *Managing the Atom Working Paper*, 2009–14, Harvard Kennedy School.

Lantis, J. S. (2002). Strategic Culture and National Security Policy. *International Security Review*, 4, 87–113.

Lavoy, P. (1995). The Strategic Consequences of Nuclear Proliferation: A Review Essay. *Security Studies*, 4/4, 695–753.

Legro, J. W. (1995). *Cooperation Under Fire*. Ithaca and London: Cornell University Press.

Luckham, R. (1984). The Armament Culture. *Alternatives*, 10, 1–44.

Mearsheimer, J. (Summer 1990). Back to the Future: Instability in Europe After the Cold War. *International Security*, 15/1, 5–56.

Mearsheimer, J. (2000, March 23). India Needs the Bomb. *The New York Times*. https://www.nytimes.com/2000/03/24/opinion/india-needs-the-bomb.html. Accessed 16 February 2020.

Miller, S. (Summer 1993). The Case Against a Ukrainian Nuclear Deterrent. *Foreign Affairs*, 72/3, 67–80.

Narang, V. (2014). *Nuclear Strategy in the Modern Era*. Princeton and Oxford: Princeton University Press.

Raghavan, V. R. (Fall/Winter 2001). Limited War and Nuclear Escalation in South Asia. *The Nonproliferation Review*, 1–18.

Rajagopalan, R. (February 2006). What Is Stability-Instability Paradox? Substantial Conflicts and the Nuclear Risk in South Asia. *SASSU Research Paper*, 4, 3–12.

Rublee, M. R. (2009). *Nonproliferation Norms: Why States Choose Nuclear Restrain*. Athens and London: University of Georgia Press.

Sagan, S. (1993). *The Limits of Safety: Organizations, Accidents and Nuclear Weapons*. Princeton: Princeton University Press.

Sagan, S. (Spring 1994). The Perils of Proliferation. Organization Theory, Deterrence Theory and the Spread of Nuclear Weapons. *International Security*, 18/4, 66–107.

Sagan, S. & Waltz, K. (2003). *The Spread of Nuclear Weapons: A Debate Renewed*. New York: W. W. Norton.

Snyder, G. (1965). The Balance of Power and the Balance of Terror. In Paul Seabury (Ed.), *The Balance of Power* (pp. 185–201). Scranton: Chandler.

Snyder, J. L. (1977). *The Soviet Strategic Culture: Implications for Limited Nuclear Operations*. Santa Monica: Rand.

Thayer, B. (Spring 1994). The Risk of Nuclear Inadvertence: A Review Essay. *Security Studies*, 3/3, 428–493.

van Creveld, M. (1993). *Nuclear Proliferation and the Future of Conflict*. New York: Free Press.

Waltz, K. (1981). The Spread of Nuclear Weapons: More May Better. *Adelphi Papers*, 171. London: International Institute for Strategic Studies.

Watterson, C. (2017). Competing Interpretations of the Stability-Instability Paradox: The Case of the Kargil War. *The Nonproliferation Review*, 24/1–2, 83–99.

Welch, S. (1993). *The Concept of Political Culture*. London: The Macmillan Press.

Weltman, J. (Winter 1981/1982). Managing Nuclear Multipolarity. *International Security*, 6/3, 182–194.

India-Pakistan Nuclear Escalation- Where Could It Lead. (2019, August 29). *Nature*, https://www.nature.com/articles/d41586-019-02578-5. Accessed 2 September 2019.

The Rediff Interview with General Ved Prakash Malik, Part 1. (2001, July 26). Crossing the LoC Would Have Hade Other Implications, Rediff.com, https://m.rediff.com/news/2001/jul/26inter.htm. Accessed 20 June 2019.

The Rediff Interview with General Ved Prakash Malik, Part 3. (2001, July 28). Kargil Was a Good Wake-up Call. Rediff.com. https://m.rediff.com/news/2001/jul/28inter.htm. Accessed 20 June 2019.

Three Models of Nuclear Weaponization Influence and Their Origins

Abstract How do countries interpret and respond to threats based on the distribution of relative power? How do countries respond to a change in the distribution of relative power? How can one explain the differences in the countries' behavior in response to a similar change? The main concern in this book is associated with the interpretation and response by countries to the change in the distribution of relative power in view of nuclear weaponization. Why nuclear weaponization differently affects the countries' military behavior during wars? Three models of nuclear weaponization are an outcome of the interpretation of changes in the distribution of relative power. Prior to elaborating the models of weaponization influence, we commence the discussion with the presentation of a causal mechanism that on the basis thereof countries interpret and respond to strategic threats and shifts in relative power distribution. Subsequently, we elaborate three models of nuclear weaponization influence on the countries' patterns of warfighting.

Keywords *Aggression Encouragement* · *Nuclear Ignorance* ·
Offensive realism · Relative material power · *Restraint Imposition* ·
Strategic culture

How do countries interpret and respond to threats based on the distribution of relative power? How do countries respond to a change in the distribution

© The Author(s) 2020
I. Davidzon, *Patterns of Conventional Warfighting under the Nuclear Umbrella*,
https://doi.org/10.1007/978-3-030-45594-1_3

of relative power? How can one explain the differences in the countries' conduct in response to a similar change? The main concern in this book is associated with the interpretation and response by countries to the change in the distribution of relative power in view of nuclear weaponization. Why nuclear weaponization differently affects the countries' military behavior during wars? Three models of nuclear weaponization are an outcome of the interpretation of changes in the distribution of relative power. Prior to elaborating the models of weaponization influence, we commence the discussion with the presentation of a causal mechanism that on the basis thereof countries interpret and respond to strategic threats and shifts in relative power distribution. Subsequently, we elaborate three models of nuclear weaponization influence on the countries' patterns of warfighting.

For the purposes of exploring a variable impact of nuclear weaponization on warfighting patterns, we implement an analysis model based on the following two variables: external variable of pre-existing strategic threat and an internal variable of strategic culture. As mentioned above, this approach is inspired by the neoclassical theory of realism. Similar to other versions of realism, neoclassical realism assumes that politics is a constant struggle between states for the division of material power and security in a world of scarce resources and widespread uncertainty.[1]

John Mearsheimer, the representative of offensive realism similarly argued that countries are concerned regarding the distribution of power among them.[2] Nevertheless, the difference between the neoclassical realism theory and other realistic approaches is a combination of both external and internal variables. Offensive realism, for instance, views the world as Hobbesian, a world in which states strive to achieve security by maximizing their relative advantage. States must adopt a policy of aggression and expansion in order to maximize power and increase influence at the expense of others. It assumes that the interests, behavior of a state are determined directly by its relative power *vis-à-vis* other countries.[3] According to Mearsheimer:

[1] Jeffrey Taliaferro, Steven Lobell, & Norrin Ripsman (2009). Introduction, in Jeffrey Taliaferro, Steven Lobell, & Norrin Ripsman (Eds.), *Neoclassical Realism, the State, and Foreign Policy*, Cambridge: Cambridge University Press, 4.

[2] John Mearsheimer (2014). *The Tragedy of Great Power Politics*, New York and London: W. W. Norton, 26.

[3] Fareed Zakaria (1998). *From Wealth to Power: The Unusual Origins of America's World Role*, Princeton: Princeton University Press, 9.

The stronger a state is relative to its potential rivals, the less likely it is that any of those will attack it and threaten its survival. Weaker states will be reluctant to pick fights with more powerful states because the weaker states are likely to suffer military defeat. Indeed, the bigger the gap in power between any two states, the less likely it is that the weaker will attack the stronger.[4]

The specific characteristics of the states play in fact no role and do not affect the way of conduct in the international arena generally and during wars, in particular. Different strategic cultures may exist but they are not likely to play any significant role.[5] To understand such behavior, one should examine the relative power and external environment of the state.[6] Nevertheless, classical realists, who appear to address different elements of material power, such as size of armies, territories of countries, and economic parameters, are unable to explain why a country chooses to act in one way or another in an international environment. The fact that the classical realism is detached from internal variables leads to a deterministic assessment of state interaction patterns: the weaker the state compared to its enemies, the less likely it is to adopt an offensive strategy and vice versa, the stronger the state compared to its enemies, the more likely it is to adopt an offensive action.

Moreover, classical realism deals with system issues, such as the probability of war outbreaking, arms races, etc. Neoclassical realism, however, constitutes a foreign policy analysis theory that deals with issues in the external environment of the states.[7] Warfighting patterns are an expression of a foreign policy during wars. A foreign policy theory, however, which is limited solely to external factors, is likely to be inaccurate. In order to understand how states interpret and respond to a security reality, one should examine how external pressure is transmitted through unit level intervening variables, such as decision-makers' perceptions.[8]

---

[4] Mearsheimer, *The Tragedy of Great Power Politics*, 26.

[5] Colin Dueck (2006). *Reluctant Crusaders: Power, Culture and Change in American Grand* Strategy, Princeton and Oxford: Princeton University Press, 17.

[6] Gideon Rose (October 1998). Neoclassical Realism and Theories of Foreign Policy, *World Politics*, 51/1, 149.

[7] Zakaria, *From Wealth to Power*, 14.

[8] Rose, Neoclassical Realism and Theories of Foreign Policy, 152.

The neoclassical realism focuses on the unit, state level and thus more suitable for analysis of countries' military behavior patterns:

> Phenomena such as individual states' grand strategies, military doctrines, foreign economic policies, alliance preferences, and crisis behavior fall within neoclassical realism's purview.[9]

A foreign policy theory cannot ignore internal factors, such as culture.[10] Gideon Rose defined this theoretical concept as follows:

> It explicitly incorporates both external and internal variables, updating and systematizing certain insights drawn from classical realist thought. Its adherents argue that the scope and ambition of a country's foreign policy is driven first and foremost by its place in the international system and specifically by its relative material power capabilities. This is why they are realist. They argue further, however, that the impact of such power capabilities on foreign policy is indirect and complex, because systemic pressures must be translated through intervening variables at the unit level. This is why they are neoclassical.[11]

As opposed to the basic assumption that states seek security, the neoclassical realists argue that states seek to cope with the uncertainty of international anarchy by controlling and shaping their external environment. Accordingly, the more resources a country has (i.e., relative power), the greater is its motivation to expand its influence on its external environment. The superpowers, in comparison to smaller countries, have more resources, interests, and goals in relation to their external environment.[12] Therefore, the more relatively powerful a country is, the more likely it is to seek to minimize the uncertainty surrounding it in relation with others by taking more aggressive, offensive actions and vice versa, the less powerful country will adopt more restrained behavior and defensive strategy. As Michael Mandelbaum mentioned:

---

[9] Jeffrey Taliaferro (Winter 2000/2001). Security Seeking Under Anarchy: Defensive Realism Revisited, *International Security*, 23/3, 134.

[10] Zakaria, *From Wealth to Power*, 16.

[11] Rose, Neoclassical Realism and Theories of Foreign Policy, 146.

[12] Kalevi Holsti (1992). *International Politics: A Framework for Analysis*, Englewood Cliffs, NJ: Prentice Hall, 276.

They [states] expand. They send their soldiers, ships, and private agents abroad. They fight wars, guard borders, and administer territories and people of different languages, customs, and beliefs far from their own capitals. They exert influence on foreigners in a variety of ways. The influence is not reciprocal. The strong do to others what others cannot do to them.[13]

Every state, in order to survive in anarchy, without a universal authority to regulate interstate relations, relies on its own capabilities. Therefore, the main criterion that will define the behavior of each state and influence international relations is the division of power among the countries.[14] The distribution of power within the international system expands or reduces the selection of strategies or options available to each country.

Nevertheless, neoclassical realism assumes that relative material power does not directly affect states' behavior but indirectly: decisions are made by leaders, decision-makers, and therefore what is actually relevant, is not necessarily the amount of available resources or power but the perception of relative power by the decision-makers.[15] In other words, the interpretation of strategic threat. The influence of relative power on countries' behavior is transmitted via decision-makers' perceptions or as Randal Schweller mentioned:

> Aside from domestic politics... threat perception is a crucial intervening variable between changes in relative power and reaction in the form of balancing behavior.[16]

A perception is not stand alone but is derived from strategic culture. Yet how is its influence on the conventional warfighting pattern implemented? As abovementioned, strategic culture consists of two parts: symbolic and operational levels. The symbolic level comprises of beliefs and assumptions regarding geostrategic environment, the country's

---

[13]Michael Mandelbaum (1989). *The Fate of Nations: The Search for National Security in the Nineteenth and Twentieth Centuries*, Cambridge: Cambridge University Press, 134–135.

[14]William Curti Wohlforth (1993). *The Elusive Balance: Power and Perceptions During the Cold War*, Ithaca: Cornell University Press, 2.

[15]Wohlforth, *The Elusive Balance*, 147.

[16]Randal Schweller (2008). *Unanswered Threats: Political Constraints on the Balance of Power*, Princeton and Oxford: Princeton University Press, 37.

self-image, and the threat posed by the enemy. In the process of choosing a certain warfighting pattern, decision-makers rely upon predetermined beliefs and assumptions on the symbolic level in order to interpret strategic threat and act upon a mass of incoming information.[17] Strategic culture forms the countries' military behavior at the operational level. Based on the beliefs at the symbolic level, the operational level refers to assumptions regarding the efficiency of available patterns of warfighting. The operational level determines which options are efficient and acceptable at the symbolic level. It excludes certain patterns of behavior as inconsistent with beliefs and assumptions at the symbolic level. Accordingly, the selection of countries' behavior patterns during wars is consistent with cultural perceptions of decision-makers. Decision-makers choose the preferred policy and behavioral pattern from the available range of options.[18]

STRATEGIC THREAT AND ITS PERCEPTION—OPERATIONALIZATION

What are the factors which constitute the basis of countries' readiness for threats? How scholars measure military power of one country versus another. How can one examine relative power relations among countries? Or quoting Michael Beckley "what makes some countries more powerful than others?"[19] How scholars can examine a relative power perception?

Power is the ability of a country to affect world politics in accordance with its interests.[20] In other words, power is a set of capabilities, certain resources available to a country for affecting other countries.[21] In this sense, power is defined as the possession of resources. This approach of possession, control over resources is commonly used by scholars to measure national power.[22] Nevertheless, countries didn't exist in a kind

---

[17] Dueck, *Reluctant Crusaders*, 14.

[18] Holsti, *International Politics*, 269–271.

[19] Michael Beckley (Fall 2018). The Power of Nations: Measuring What Matters, *International Security*, 43/2, 7.

[20] Beckley, The Power of Nations, 8.

[21] Joseph Ney (Summer 1990). The Changing Nature of World Power, *Political Science Quarterly*, 105/2, 178.

[22] Jeffrey Hart (Spring 1976). Three Approaches to the Measurement of Power in International Relations, *International Organization*, 30/2, 289. See also: Hans

of vacuum. They exist in an international system characterized by many interfaces among countries, both friendly and rival. As Kenneth Waltz noted:

> Although states are like unites functionally, they differ vastly in their capabilities.[23]

Accordingly, what is relevant is not the resources of a country as such but rather a relative power, balance of power among the same and other countries, especially hostile ones. Therefore, power is a distribution of capabilities among countries.[24] The more resources a country has, i.e., greater relative power compared to others, the greater the capability thereof to influence its external environment, than countries with fewer resources at their disposal. Traditionally, scholars measured national power according to such parameters as natural resources, population, armed forces, and gross national product.[25] According to Waltz, countries' capabilities include size of population and territory, resource endowment, economic capability, military strength, political stability, and competence.[26]

Since this book deals with the military behavior of the countries, we refer to three kinds of countries' relative material power resources, which are relevant to assessment of warfighting patterns: geostrategic situation, the size of armed forces and militaries' budgets. Assessment and comparison of resources of country A versus country B form pre-existing strategic threat and are the basis for countries' decision to choose one warfighting pattern or another.

Morgenthau (1967). *Politics Among Nations*, New York: Alfred A. Knopf; Klaus Knorr (1956). *The War Potential of Nations*, Princeton: Princeton University Press.

[23] Kenneth Waltz (2010). *Theory of International Politics*, Long Grove: Waveland Press, Inc., 105.

[24] Waltz, *Theory of International Politics*, 192.

[25] Ashley Tellis, Janice Bially, Christopher Layne, & Melissa McPherson (2000). *Measuring National Power in the Postindustrial Age*, Santa Monica: RAND Corporation, 14.

[26] Waltz, *Theory of International Politics*, 131.

Geostrategy Situation

Geostrategy is the relationship between geography and war management programs. Geostrategy affects the conditions and capabilities of a country to wage a war.[27] Geographical, environmental conditions are central to the adoption of a warfighting pattern. While discussing the power definition and its measurement, Mearsheimer addressed also geographical dimensions and argued:

> First, land power is a dominant form of military power in the modern world… Second, large bodies of water profoundly limit the power-projection capabilities of land forces.[28]

The better the country's geostrategic conditions, the greater its relative power. A country with a convenient geography, such as the presence of wide areas that provide strategic depth, will benefit from a clear advantage *vis-à-vis* a small country lacking territorial depth. Thus, for instance, a country with large territories, such as Russia, can conduct war even by using an attrition strategy, drawing the enemy into its territorial depth, in order to concentrate enough force for a counterattack. On the other hand, a country with small territory may find it difficult to adopt strategies that involve the risk of losing control, even temporarily, over part of the territory. Smaller countries cannot trade off a land against organization time for defense and offensive.[29]

Size of Armed Forces

Size of a military manpower is the second kind of resource providing assessment of the country's relative power. First, an assessment of military manpower yields useful information regarding the relative mass of raw power, which a country is able to deploy in a war.[30] Second, this data is important in analyzing countries' preference regarding

[27] Tal Tovy (2015). *The Changing Nature of Geostrategy 1900–2000: The Evolution of a New Paradigm*, Maxwell Air Force Base, AL: Air Force Research Institute, 27.

[28] Mearsheimer, *The Tragedy of Great Power Politics*, Chapter Four.

[29] Tovy, *The Changing Nature of Geostrategy 1900–2000*, 28.

[30] Ashley Tellis, Janice Bially, Christopher Layne, & Melissa McPherson, *Measuring National Power*, 138.

warfighting. In contrast to countries with smaller armies, countries with larger armies have the advantage of deploying, if necessary, units in a wider geographical area, such as fighting concurrently at more than one front at a time. This is in addition to the ability to maintain and reinforce combat units over time. On the contrary, it would be difficult for countries with smaller armies to deploy military units at more than one front at a time.

Military Budgets

The size of the military budget is the third kind of resource yielding insight the into country's relative power. Assessing the size of a military budget provides an assessment of the amount of resources a country is capable of allocating to its own army. The economic component of relative power is the basis for the maintenance of armed forces according to security needs. It is the expression of the national economic power. The stronger the economic base, the more resources, compared to others, a country could allocate to its army and vice versa: a weak economic base and economic difficulties affect a state's ability to allocate adequate resources to military needs. In order to analyze the military budgets of the three case studies we use data revealing the size of the country's military budgets.

Cultural Images

Decision-makers are socialized in a strategic culture and perceive reality through cultural images. Cultural beliefs and assumptions are repeated over time. They become a kind of filter that sorts behavior patterns according to their compatibility with the respective cultural predisposition. Therefore, it becomes difficult to consider alternatives which are not compliant with cultural assumptions.[31] As noted aforementioned, the effect of culture on behavior is expressed at the operative level, which is derived from the symbolic level. In view of the foregoing, in order to examine the causal relationship between strategic culture and behavior and to predict probable warfighting pattern, one is required to look for assumptions concerning effective patterns as prescribed by attitudes at

---

[31] Dueck, *Reluctant Crusaders*, 15.

the symbolic level of strategic culture.[32] We assume that these attitudes are formed not with regard to strategic conditions from distant historical periods but, mainly, from the modern history, which is more relevant to a country's political–military situation.

If there is a congruence over time in preference of some pattern of behavior, then the strategic culture exists and presents up to the present.[33] Accordingly, to examine these assumptions and attitudes regarding warfighting patterns, we analyze statements made by political and military leaders and articles and books written by them addressing issues of military strategy. In light of the fact that this study deals with warfighting patterns during conventional wars, it refers to a period of time between declaration of independence by the three examined countries and the last conventional war fought by India, Israel, and Pakistan—Yom Kippur war in 1973 in the Israeli case and Kargil war in 1999 in the Indian and Pakistani cases.

Three Models of Nuclear Weaponization Effect

Crossing the threshold of a nuclear weaponization could alter decision-makers' perception of relative power. The nuclear weapon introduction could be perceived differently by decision-makers in different countries. State A could perceive the entry of nuclear weapons as a change in power relations, as a form of compensation for the conventional supremacy of state B and as a defense against the threat it poses. At the same time, although state B can also have a nuclear arsenal, but perceives the obtaining of nuclear weapons by its weaker rival as a change in relative power. In other words, in each case nuclear weaponization indeed shall affect relative power perception. Nevertheless, it is possible that a country acquires nuclear weapons but does not perceive such a significant increase in its force as a change in the balance of power *vis-à-vis* its rivals. Despite the existence of nuclear capability, such a state ignores it and does not interpret it as changing the conventional power relations with its adversaries. Thus, weaponization doesn't change its traditional patterns of warfighting: it neither encourages offensive military behavior nor imposes restraint and deters a country to act offensively and escalate a conflict.

---

[32] Johnston, *Cultural Realism*, 37.

[33] Johnston, *Cultural Realism*, 40.

Hence, introduction of new devastating weapon technology, i.e., nuclear weapon, affects differently the countries' patterns of conventional warfighting. While the beliefs and attitudes at the symbolic level of strategic culture are constant, nuclear weaponization could cause either to a persistence of the existing preferred patterns of warfighting or to change and adopt a new preferred one in terms of existing strategic culture.

In order to determine whether nuclear weapons influenced or altered (if at all) the pattern of warfare, a comparison must be made in respect of the warfighting pattern in conventional wars before nuclear weaponization and thereafter. Therefore, we argue that in the pre-weaponization period a weaker country with the perception of power inferiority *vis-à-vis* a stronger enemy and/or revisionist beliefs resulting from political–territorial dispute is more likely to prefer an offensive and aggressive pattern of warfighting with a tendency to escalate during a war. A stronger country, with the perception of power superiority *vis-à-vis* a weaker, even aggressive, revisionist enemy, is more likely to adopt a defensive and restrained, at least at the beginning of the conflict, warfighting pattern, with tendency to act offensively after the start of the war.

In the interstate conflict with the mutual possession of nuclear weapons, the strategic culture-based perception of relative material power allows to predict the nuclear weaponization influence according to the following models:

- *Aggression Encouragement*: A weaker one, with the perception of power inferiority *vis-à-vis* enemy and/or revisionist beliefs will perceive a nuclear weapon acquisition as a change of relative power and as a form of "force multiplier." Nuclear weapon acquisition will encourage the respective party to persist with the existing pattern of offensive and escalating warfighting. Nuclear weaponization is perceived as a means of defense against a conventionally superior enemy. In other words, a change in relative power perception is expressed in the ability under the nuclear umbrella to preserve the preferred warfighting patterns consistent with the strategic culture.
- *Restraint Imposition*: A stronger state will perceive an introduction of a nuclear weapon into the conflict as a restrain imposition factor, due to the possession of the nuclear weapon by the revisionist, aggressive enemy. Nuclear weaponization will change the relative

power perception while adjusting the preferred warfighting pattern under the existing strategic culture. Following the change in the perception of relative power, the state will prefer adopting a defensive pattern of warfighting but without escalation in the course of a war. In other words, nuclear weaponization will change the conventional warfighting pattern: from defensive with an escalation element during a war to defensive with restraint element during hostilities.

We can identify, in this respect, another kind of paradox, the "Weak-Strong Actors Paradox," in which the weaker side gets an advantage over the strong side. According to Kapur:

> Nuclear weapons would afford the weaker state a shield against its advisory's superior conventional military capabilities. If the strong state ever threatened the weak state with catastrophic military defeat, the weak state could respond with a nuclear attack... the danger of a nuclear response would constrain the strong state, making it much less likely to launch a full-scale conventional attack against its adversary.

In the interstate conflict with the possession of nuclear weapon only by one state, the nuclear weaponization effect on this country's warfighting pattern is predicted according to the third model of *Nuclear Ignorance*:

- *Nuclear "Ignorance"*: A country which crossed nuclear weaponization threshold and exclusively possesses nuclear arsenal will not necessarily perceive the acquired nuclear capability as a change of relative power *vis-à-vis* its stronger enemies at the conventional level. As long as the conflict remains at the conventional level, the state will not see nuclear weapons as an alternative or a compensation to its conventional inferior capabilities. Under such circumstances, the state's warfighting preferences or changes thereof are detached from nuclear weaponization. This means that such a country will remain with the existing warfighting pattern.

REFERENCES

Beckley, M. (Fall 2018). The Power of Nations: Measuring What Matters. *International Security*, 43/2, 7–44.

Dueck, C. (2006). *Reluctant Crusaders: Power, Culture and Change in American Grand Strategy*. Princeton and Oxford: Princeton University Press.

Hart, J. (Spring 1976). Three Approaches to the Measurement of Power in international Relations. *International Organization*, 30/2, 289–305.

Holsti, K. (1992). *International Politics: A Framework for Analysis*. Englewood Cliffs, NJ: Prentice Hall.

Johnston, A. I. (1995). *Cultural Realism: Strategic Culture and Grand Strategy in Chinese History*. Princeton, NJ: Princeton University Press.

Knorr, K. (1956). *The War Potential of Nations*. Princeton: Princeton University Press.

Mearsheimer, J. (2014). *The Tragedy of Great Power Politics*. New York and London: W. W. Norton.

Morgenthau, H. (1967). *Politics Among Nations*. New York: Alfred A. Knopf.

Ney, J. (Summer 1990). The Changing Nature of World Power. *Political Science Quarterly*, 105/2, 177–192.

Rose, G. (October 1998). Neoclassical Realism and Theories of Foreign Policy. *World Politics*, 51/1, 144–172.

Schweller, R. (2008). *Unanswered Threats: Political Constraints on the Balance of Power*. Princeton and Oxford: Princeton University Press.

Taliaferro, J. (Winter 2000/2001). Security Seeking Under Anarchy: Defensive Realism Revisited. *International Security*, 23/3, 128–161.

Taliaferro, J., Lobell, S., & Ripsman, N. (2009). Introduction. In Jeffrey Taliaferro, Steven Lobell, & Norrin Ripsman (Eds.), *Neoclassical Realism, the State, and Foreign Policy* (pp. 1–41). Cambridge: Cambridge University Press.

Tellis, A., Bially, J., Layne, C., & McPherson, M. (2000). *Measuring National Power in the Postindustrial Age*. Santa Monica: RAND Corporation.

Tovy, T. (2015). *The Changing Nature of Geostrategy 1900–2000: The Evolution of a New Paradigm*. Maxwell Air Force Base, AL: Air Force Research Institute.

Waltz, K. (2010). *Theory of International Politics*. Long Grove: Waveland Press, Inc.

Wohlforth, W. C. (1993). *The Elusive Balance: Power and Perceptions During the Cold War*. Ithaca: Cornell University Press.

Zakaria, F. (1998). *From Wealth to Power: The Unusual Origins of America's World Role*. Princeton: Princeton University Press.

CHAPTER 4

The Relative Power and Its Perception

Abstract What are the pre-existing strategic threats that Pakistan, India, and Israel have faced? How these threats are perceived by the political and military decision-makers in these countries? How these perceptions affect the warfighting preference of their armies? How nuclear weaponization affected their fighting patterns? To address these questions, we start with a brief review of the pre-existing strategic threats of the countries, which consist of relative material power components *vis-à-vis* their adversaries: the countries' geostrategic situation, size of the armies, and the budgets allocated to defense purposes. Then, we proceed with the review of the strategic cultures, through which the Pakistani, Indian, and Israeli decision-makers perceive the strategic threats. We continue the discussion by presenting the warfighting patterns, which derived from the strategic culture beliefs and attitudes and adopted by the three armies in the pre-weaponization period. As demonstrated below, different threat interpretation could cause adoption of similar patterns of warfighting. Subsequently, we analyze the nuclear weaponization effect on the patterns of conventional warfighting, as expressed by the three weaponization influence models, i.e., *Aggression Encouragement, Restraint Imposition, and Nuclear "Ignorance"*.

Keywords Geostrategic situation · Military budgets · Siege mentality · Size of military · Threat perception · Two-nation theory

© The Author(s) 2020   47
I. Davidzon, *Patterns of Conventional
Warfighting under the Nuclear Umbrella*,
https://doi.org/10.1007/978-3-030-45594-1_4

What are the pre-existing strategic threats that Pakistan, India, and Israel have faced? How these threats are perceived by the political and military decision-makers in these countries? How these perceptions affect the warfighting preference of their armies? How nuclear weaponization affected their fighting patterns? To address these questions, we start with a brief review of the pre-existing strategic threats of the countries, which consist of relative material power components *vis-à-vis* their adversaries: the countries' geostrategic situation, size of the armies, and the budgets allocated to defense purposes. Then, we proceed with the review of the strategic cultures, through which the Pakistani, Indian, and Israeli decision-makers perceive the strategic threats. We continue the discussion by presenting the warfighting patterns, which derived from the strategic culture beliefs and attitudes and adopted by the three armies in the pre-weaponization period. As demonstrated below, different threat interpretation could cause adoption of similar patterns of warfighting.

Subsequently, we analyze the nuclear weaponization effect on the patterns of conventional warfighting, as expressed by the three weaponization influence models, i.e., *Aggression Encouragement, Restraint Imposition, and Nuclear "Ignorance"*.

PAKISTAN

Geostrategic Situation

Pakistan borders several countries: in the west—Iran and Afghanistan, at the northeast it has a common border with China, and in the south lies Pakistan on the shores of the Arabian Sea. Finally, in the east it shares a border with India. Before 1971, when the country was divided into two parts, separated by Indian territory, its eastern part, now the state of Bangladesh, was almost completely encircled by India. Given the history of conflict with India, We will focus on the analysis of the geostrategic situation of Islamabad in the context of the Indian military challenge.

Dr. Shaukatullah Ansari, a public figure of Muslim origin in British India, predicted two years prior to Pakistani independence in his 1945 book "Pakistan: The Problem of India," that under the geostrategic conditions that would be created, the new Muslim state would find it difficult to defend its borders.[1]

Almost two years prior to Pakistan's proclamation of the independence, the Chief of General Staff in British India, General Arthur F. Smith, stated that a new country will lack a strategic depth.[2] Indeed, the essential characteristic of the geostrategic situation of Pakistan is a lack of strategic depth. Strategic depth is the country's inner geographical space between the front line and its vital territory, such as population centers or industrial areas. One of the senior generals in the Pakistani army described the problematic situation of the state as follows:

> Pakistan is narrow, that is from north to south our lines of communication, our industrial centers, our towns, our major cities lie fairly close to a country [India] that is not very friendly with us, and with which we have a border that has no geographical impediments.[3]

Most of the Pakistani communication lines are located parallel to the border with India. Furthermore, most of the largest cities in Pakistan are close to the Indian border.[4] Lahore, the capital of the province of Punjab, for instance, is only 60 km away from the Indian border. Additionally, the port city of Karachi is also close to the border with India, and thus exposed to the land, air, and naval threat of the Indian armed forces. This creates a constraint on Pakistan's military deployment against its great enemy. Pakistani officers assumed that the confrontation with India could escalate quickly without sufficient defense forces being deployed in the relevant geographic area.[5] Compared to the geostrategic situation of India, as shall be detailed below, there is undoubtedly an asymmetry between the two countries in favor of New Delhi: India has

[1] Shaukatullah Ansari (1945). *Pakistan: The Problem of India*, Lahore: Minerva Book Shop, 70.

[2] Cited in Ashish Shukla (July–September 2011). Pakistan's Quest for Strategic Depth: Regional Security Implications, *Himalayan and Central Asian Studies*, 15/3, 85.

[3] Cited in Stephen Cohen (1984). *The Pakistan Army*, Berkeley and Los Angeles: University of California Press, 141–142.

[4] Pervaiz Iqbal Cheema (2002). *The Armed Forces of Pakistan*, New York: New York University Press, 3.

[5] Cohen, *The Pakistani Army*, 143.

about three times more depth than Pakistan and the proportional average depth of Pakistan compared to India is minor.[6]

Furthermore, before the establishment of Bangladesh, after the Indo-Pak war of 1971, the geographic distance between the two parts of the country, west and east, also contributed to the complex geostrategic situation. The Indian "barrier," that separated the two country's parts, made it difficult to protect the eastern part, which, as mentioned, was almost completely surrounded by Indian territory. Under these circumstances, the Pakistanis made a decision to abandon the defense of this region, as during the war in 1965.[7] Nevertheless, during the war in 1971 the scenario of a direct Indian attack on the eastern part of the country was materialized. Ironically, the loss of the eastern part of Pakistan improved its geostrategic situation in the sense that that the army did not have to take into account any longer the possibility of splitting forces to protect the two parts of the country. Thus, the challenge to conduct a two-fronts war with India has been removed.[8]

It should be noted that Pakistan's policy toward Afghanistan was also influenced by the Indian threat, namely Pakistan's fear of New Delhi's rapprochement with Kabul that could militarily threaten Islamabad. This concern is evident, for example, in the attitude of the former Pakistani leader, Mohammad Ayub Khan (1958–1969):

> …the Afghans were backed by India whose interest lay in ensuring that in the event of a war with us over Kashmir, the Afghans should open a second front against Pakistan on the North-West Frontier.[9]

Deriving from the prism of the Indian threat, Pakistanis pursue the goal of minimizing the Indian influence in this unstable country.[10] Pakistan, aiming to maintain friendly relationships with the Afghan government,

[6] Lt. Col. Khalid Masood Khan (2015, October 16). The Strategic Depth Concept, *The Nation*, https://nation.com.pk/16-Oct-2015/the-strategic-depth-concept. Accessed 6 July 2019.

[7] Khan, *Eating Grass*, 46.

[8] Feroz Hassan Khan (September 2015). Going Tactical: Pakistan's Nuclear Posture and Implications for Stability, *Proliferation Paper*, 53, 27.

[9] Mohammad Ayub Khan (2008). *Friends Not Masters*, Dhaka: The University Press Limited, 174–175.

[10] Marvin Weinbaum & Jonathan Harder (March 2008). Pakistan's Afghan Policies and Their Consequences, *Contemporary South Asia*, 16/1, 26.

sees its territory as a form of alternative strategic depth.[11] Politicly, the end of strategic depth is the cultivation of a friendly regime in Kabul to prevent the development of a close relationship between Afghanistan and India.[12] From a geostrategic point of view, the probable purpose of using the Afghan territory as a strategic depth is to ensure the Pakistani army's ability, and if necessary, to retreat to the territory of the neighboring country for the organization of counterattack against Indian forces.[13]

Size of Pakistani Military

The military threats, mainly posed by India, forced Pakistan to increase its military forces. In absolute terms, Pakistan has significant military forces. Nevertheless, in comparison to India, the Pakistani military suffers from a substantial quantitative asymmetry. This trend was already evident as of the early days of the country's independence and this quantitative asymmetry has been maintained for decades over an average of 1–2 in favor of India. This asymmetry is even intensified if one takes into consideration the long border with India which the military is required to defend.

The partition plan between India and Pakistan, administered by the British colonial government, also included the division of the British Imperial India Army between two new political entities. Thus, Pakistanis received 4 out of 6 armored divisions, 8 out of 40 artillery divisions, and 8 out of 15 infantry brigades.[14] Since then, the army has evolved and, as can be seen from the chart below, its size has almost constantly increased (with the exception of a slight decrease in 1985). A significant quantitative increase of more than 100,000 soldiers can be identified in 1975, most probably due to the severe consequences of the third Indo-Pakistan war for Islamabad. In 2016 the growth trend reached a peak of 615,000 military personnel (see Fig. 4.1).

---

[11] Aidan Parkes (2019). Considered Chaos: Revisiting Pakistan's "Strategic Depth" in Afghanistan, *Strategic Studies*, 3.

[12] Christine Fair (2014). *Fighting to the End: The Pakistanis Army Way of War*, New York: Oxford University Press, 103.

[13] Larry Hanauer & Peter Chalk (2012). *India's and Pakistan's Strategies in Afghanistan*, Santa Monica: RAND Center for Asia Pacific Policy, 26.

[14] Shuja Nawaz (2008). *Crossed Swords: Pakistan, Its Army, and the Wars Within*, Oxford: Oxford University Press, 32.

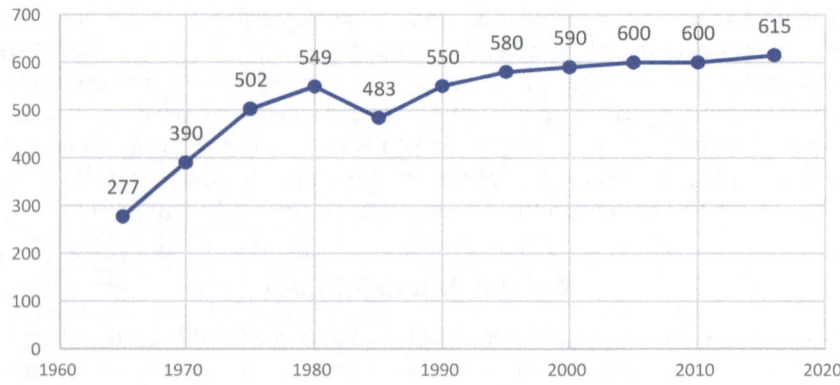

Fig. 4.1 Pakistani military (thousands) (*Source* World Military Expenditures and Arms Transfers, http://www.state.gov/t/avc/rls/rpt/wmeat. Accessed 28 August 2019)

Pakistan's Military Budget

One of the main characteristics of the national budget of Islamabad is the high defense expenditure. As Feroz Hassan Khan noted:

> Pakistan's top national security issue and challenge is its economic security, without which the country would not be able to modernize its national security which is imperative for survival.[15]

This trend has already taken place in 1947.[16] The considerable part of Pakistan's defense expenditure can undoubtedly be explained by the

---

[15] Pakistan Should Protect Its National Interest over Middle East Crisis (2020, January 7). *DAWN*, https://www.dawn.com/news/1526716/pakistan-should-protect-its-national-interest-over-middle-east-crisis. Accessed 8 January 2020.

[16] Ayesha Siddiqa-Agha (2001). *Pakistan's Arms Procurement and Military Buildup, 1979–99*, New York: Palgrave, 79.

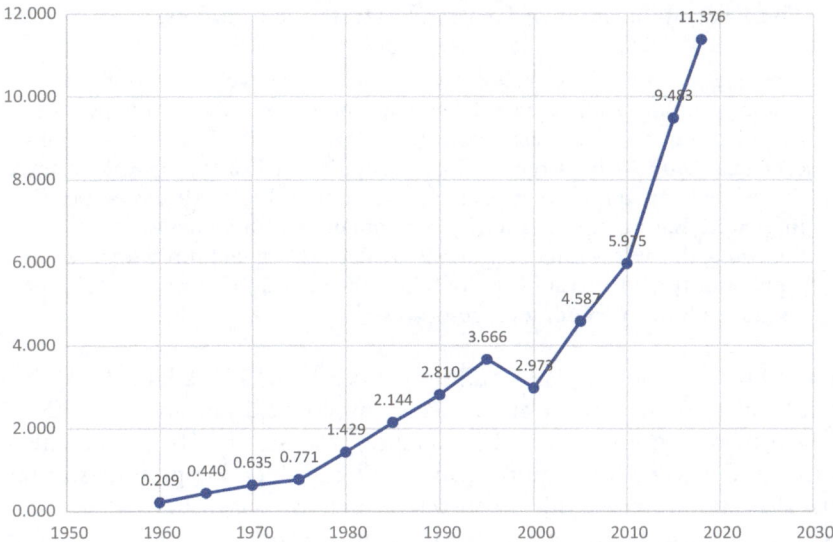

Fig. 4.2 Pakistan's military expenditure, billions (USD) (*Source* World Bank Data, https://data.worldbank.org/indicator/MS.MIL.XPND.CD. Accessed 26 November 2019)

major threat posed by India, as perceived by Islamabad.[17] In 1948–1955, defense spending was twice the cost of civilian development.[18] Since then, the country's defense budget has steadily increased (see Fig. 4.2). Pakistan's military failures in wars against India have contributed to the increase in military expenditure.[19] While in the 1960s, Islamabad's military expenditure was almost half billion dollars (USD), in 1970 it increased to over $600 million.

---

[17] Siddiqa-Agha, *Pakistan's Arms Procurement and Military Buildup, 1979–99*, 190.

[18] Parvez Hassan (2007, January 22). State and Pakistan Economy: Where Have We Come From? Where Do We Go? www.economyofpakistan.blogspot.com/2007/01/state-and-pakistan-economy-where-have_22.html. Accessed 25 November 2019.

[19] Nawaz, *Crossed Swords*, 27.

The Pakistani economist Parvez Hassan stated as follows:

The biggest impact of 1965 war was to change the priorities of public spending. Indeed, real defense spending rose little over 3 per cent per annum in the five years before the 1965 war with India. It is significant that Ayub Khan, a former commander-in-chief of the army, kept the size of the army under strict control, even though India's defense expenditures were raising rapidly after its confrontation with China in 1962. But following the war with India in 1965, defense expenditures were given high priority and phasing out of US military assistance after 1965 put additional burden on domestic resources.[20]

By 1980, Pakistan's defense budget has reached 1429 billion USD. The tense relations led to an arms race between Pakistan and New Delhi, which of course was reflected in defense expenses. In 2018, the defense expenditure was already more than 11 billion USD. Despite the substantial allocation of economic resources for defense purposes by Pakistan, as we will see also below, New Delhi has an advantage in defense expenditure, which only grows. This asymmetry is also reflected in the other parameters of relative power. The question is how was this asymmetry perceived by the decision-makers in Islamabad?

Strategic Culture

The dominant player in Pakistan's politics and society is its military establishment. Over the years, this dominance has been expressed both directly (military dictatorship) and indirectly, through civil rule with the active involvement of the military. This dynamic has taken root in the country since its independence.[21] Thus, the narrative of strategic culture is influenced by the perceptions and attitudes of military officers.

Pakistan's national self-image is based on the ideological foundation on which Muslims see themselves as equal to others, primarily Hindus.[22] The concept of a separate Muslim entity in the Indian subcontinent was first conceived in the 1930s by Choudhari Rahmat Ali, which advocated

[20] Hassan, State and Pakistan Economy.

[21] Fair, *Fighting to the End*, 28.

[22] Feroz Hassan Khan (November 2005). Comparative Strategic Culture: The Case of Pakistan, *Strategic Insights*, 6/10, 3.

the establishment of a federation of 10 Muslim states.[23] This idea was expressed in the two-nation theory of Muhammad Ali Jinnah. Jinnah was the leader of the Muslim League, also known as the Qayid-i-Azam, the great leader, whom Stephen Cohen, a prominent researcher and expert on security in the South Asian region, called George Washington of Pakistan.[24] According to the theory, Muslims and Hindus are two different nationalities, and therefore each is entitled to a state of its own. From the Muslim League leader's point of view, despite a long history of the shared life, nations so different from one another cannot merge into one nation within a democratic constitutional framework.[25] From the Muslims' point of view, the historical experience has shown that the Indian leadership did not seek cooperation among Hindus and Muslims on an equal basis but rather sought to conceal their separate identity.[26] Stronger supporters of Pakistan even saw the Indian caste system as an evidence of the inability to integrate Muslims and Hindus under one political framework of united India.[27] In 1940, at the Muslim League's meeting in Lahore, Jinnah presented the idea of an independent Muslim state:

...it has always been taken for granted mistakenly that the Mussalmans are a minority, and of course we have got used to it for such a long time that these settled notions are difficult to remove. The Mussalmans are nor a minority. The Mussalmans are a nation by any definition... We occupy large parts of this country where the Mussalmans are in a majority, such as Bengal, Punjab, N.W.F.P., Sind and Baluchistan...

Islam and Hinduism are not religions in the strict sense of the word, but are, in fact, different and distinct social orders; and it is a dream that the Hindus and Muslims can ever evolve a common nationality... It is quite clear that Hindus and Mussalmans derive their inspirations from different sources of history. Very often the hero of one is a foe of the other, and likewise their victories and defeats overlap. To yoke together two such

[23]Stephen Cohen (2004). *The Idea of Pakistan*, Washington, DC: The Brookings Institution, 26.

[24]Cohen, *The Idea of Pakistan*, 28.

[25]Presidential Address by Muhammad Ali Jinnah to the Muslim League, Lahore, 1940, http://columbia.edu/itc/mealac/pritchett/00islaminks/txt_jinnah_lohore_1940.html. Accessed 27 July 2019.

[26]Zulfikar Ali Bhutto (1969). *The Myth of Independence*, London: Oxford University Press, 170.

[27]Cohen, *The Idea of Pakistan*, 35.

nations under a single state, one as a numerical minority and the other as a majority, must lead to growing discontent, and final destruction of any fabric that may be so built up for the government of such a state.[28]

This attitude has become an integral part of national self-perception in Pakistan's strategic culture. Therefore, no arrangement other than the one that would provide political independence cannot guarantee the existence of the Muslim nation on the Indian subcontinent.[29] Justice is not possible for Muslims in a unified political system dominated by a Hindu majority. Therefore, the solution was to establish an independent political entity for the Muslim minority in response to its oppression by the Hindu majority. As former Pakistani Prime Minister Nawaz Sharif noted on March 16, 2017, during a speech to an assembly of representatives of the Hindu minority in the country:

Pakistan was not made so one religion can dominate over others... Pakistan's creation itself was a struggle against religion oppression.[30]

In line with such narrative, the current Prime Minister of Pakistan, Imran Khan noted in his speech On Birth Anniversary of Quaid-e-Azam:

The entire World is witnessing the perversion of the so called secular outlook of the Indian Constitution today with discrimination and brutal actions against different minorities especially Muslims, including the passage of Citizenship Act-2019 and its aftermath. Indeed, these developments have, again, vindicated the conviction of Quaid-e-Azam Muhammad Ali Jinnah that the extremist Hindus of India would never allow the Muslim minority to live with respect and.[31]

It should be emphasized that this isolationist approach, which was at the core of the idea of a separate independent state formation for the Muslim

[28] Presidential Address by Muhammad Ali Jinnah to the Muslim League, Lahore, 1940.

[29] Ishtiaq Husain Qureshi (1956). *The Pakistani Way of Life*, New York: Frederick A. Praeger, 13.

[30] Kunwar Khuldune Shahid (2017, March 16). Nawaz Sharif's Historic Holi Address, *The Diplomat*, https://thediplomat.com/2017/03/nawaz-sharifs-historic-holi-address. Accessed 28 July 2019.

[31] Message from Prime Minister Imran Khan on Birth Anniversary of Quaid-e-Azam (2019, December 25), https://www.facebook.com/ImranKhanOfficial/posts/message-ofprime-minister-of-the-islamic-republic-of-pakistanmr-imran-khanon-the-/3144165112292554. Accessed December 25, 2019.

population of the Indian subcontinent, also contributed to the sense of insecurity.[32] The main concern of Pakistanis was the collapse of the country as a result of the hostile policies of the powerful neighbor, India. The emphasis on separatism and the separate identity was a response to India's efforts to suppress a young state in its early days.[33] The antagonism between India and Pakistan was perceived as a direct continuation of the conflict of interests and mistrust between the Hindu Congress Party and the Muslim League in the pre-independence period. Former President of Pakistan, Zulfikar Ali Bhutto, stressed this point in his book "The Myth of Independence":

> The Indian Congress Party resisted the partition of the country but failed to prevent the establishment of Pakistan. It is thus natural that some Indian leaders should continue to nurture grievances against Pakistan. Only because India persists in not permitting the completion of Pakistan have relations between the two countries deteriorated into their present hopeless deadlock.[34]

Further to this view, the Indian leadership agreed upon the formation of an independent state only after realizing that based on such arrangement the British would agree to end their control over the subcontinent.[35]

The issues that arose immediately after the establishment of the state (refugees, Kashmir, water) could not be solved peacefully due to India's unwillingness to achieve such solution. According to a Pakistani scholar, Hasan Askari Rizvi, this reluctance stemmed from India's desire to endanger the very existence of Pakistan.[36] As Stephen Cohen noted:

> ...many Indian leaders were all too eager to ensure that the new state of Pakistan would have a short live... Moreover, they expected Pakistan to fail.[37]

---

[32] Hasan Askari Rizvi (2002). Pakistan's Strategic Culture, in Michael Chambers (Ed.), *South Asia in 2020: Future Strategic Balances and Alliances*, Carlisle, PA: Strategic Studies Institute, 309.

[33] Rizvi, Pakistan's Strategic Culture, 310.

[34] Bhutto, *The Myth of Independence*, 163–164.

[35] Bhutto, *The Myth of Independence*, 170.

[36] Rizvi, Pakistan's Strategic Culture, 311.

[37] Cohen, *The Idea of Pakistan*, 39.

The process of British India partition into two states, India and Pakistan, created hostility between them, which remains up to the date hereof.[38] This process was accompanied by ethnic violence between Muslims and Hindus, which sowed the seeds of hostility between the two countries and shaped the image of India as an enemy in the strategic culture of Pakistan.[39] In his memoir "In the Line of Fire," former Pakistani Army Chief of Staff and President, General Pervez Musharraf describes the tragic events of the partition in August 1947 as follows:

> These were troubled times. These were momentous times...Thousands of Muslim families left their homes and hearts in India that August... Train after the train transported then into the unknown. Many didn't make it-they were tortured, raped, and killed along the way by vengeful Sikhs and Hindus.[40]

The perception of India as an enemy appears in many of the statements by Pakistani politicians and military officers. As Muhammad Ayub Khan noted:

> ...the cause of our major problems is India's inability to reconcile herself to our existence as a sovereign, independent State. The Indian attitude can be explained only in pathological terms. The Indian leaders have a deep hatred for the Muslims... From the beginning, India was determined to make things difficult for us... At the back of it all was India's ambition to absorb Pakistan or turn her into a satellite. The Indian leaders made no secret of their designs.[41]

Zulfikar Ali Bhutto also emphasized India's expansionist aspirations as a major cause of hostility:

> In the light of these historical and psychological factors which govern the Indian attitude towards Pakistan, it is clear that Indian leaders have come

---

[38] Sumit Ganguly & Paul Kapur (2010). *India, Pakistan and the Bomb*, New York: Columbia University Press.

[39] Rizvi, Pakistan's Strategic Culture, 310.

[40] Pervez Musharraf (2006). *In the Line of Fire*, London: Simon & Shuster UK Ltd., 11–12.

[41] Khan, *Friends Not Masters*, 115.

to tolerate Pakistan, because they do not have the power to destroy her. If they could forge this power, as they endeavoring to do by the augmentation of their military resources, they would end partition and reabsorb Pakistan into the India of their dreams. They have pronounced Pakistan their chief enemy.[42]

General Pervez Musharraf similarly addressed the issue of Indo-Pakistan relations:

Quite obviously... we need to defend ourselves against Indian threat. India's intentions were offensive and aggressive; ours were defensive.[43]

A similar view is also evident among the Pakistani military. Former Pakistani Army Commander, General Ashfaq Parvez Kayani, also referred to India as a major threat:

We cannot base our strategies on any good intentions, no matter how noble they may be, as intentions can change overnight. Our strategy has to be based on India's capability.[44]

In the course of the meeting of Senate Defense Committee of the Pakistani Parliament in August 2015 with the Pakistani General Staff, headed by General Rashad Mahmoud, Pakistani officers emphasized that India poses a major military threat to Pakistan.[45] During the visit of Senate Defense Committee at Joint Staff Headquarters in Rawalpindi in July 2018, Pakistani military headed by the Chairman of Joined Chiefs of Staff Committee, General Rashad Mahmood, reiterated the perception that India should be deemed to constitute the main external threat to Pakistani security.[46]

---

[42] Bhutto, *The Myth of Independence*, 170.

[43] Musharraf, *In the Line of Fire*, 284–285.

[44] Anita Joshua (2011, October 19). Pakistan Is Not Like Iraq or Afghanistan, Kayani Tells Washington, *The Hindu*, http://www.thehindu.com/news/international/pakistan-is-not-like-iraq-or-afghanistan-kayani-tells-washington/article2551586.ece. Accessed 4 August 2019.

[45] India Is the Only External Threat, Says Military (2015, August 28). *DAWN*, https://www.dawn.com/news/1203329. Accessed 4 August 2019.

[46] India—The Only External Threat: Pakistani Military. (2018, July 12). *India Times*, https://economictimes.indiatimes.com/news/defence/india-the-only-external-threat-pakistani-military/articleshow/48707940.cms. Accessed 4 August 2019.

It should be noted that India's image as hostile to Pakistan even strengthened following the results of the third Indo-Pak war in 1971, during which, as aforementioned, Pakistan lost its eastern part.[47]

A central issue in Pakistan's strategic culture and the enmity between the two countries is the issue of Kashmir. The dispute over this area also caused three out of the four Indo-Pakistani wars.[48] On the partition eve, the Kashmir region was populated by a Muslim majority under the Hindu rule, Maharaja Hari Singh. Following the invasion of the tribal forces from Pakistan after the partition, the Hindu ruler appealed to India to seek protection. This assistance was provided by the Indian authorities in exchange for Maharaja's consent to attach Kashmir to India.[49] These developments escalated into a war between the two young states. At the end of the war, two-thirds of Kashmir territory were controlled by India and the rest remained under the Pakistani control.[50]

For the first generation of Pakistanis, the issue of Kashmir is not necessarily a matter of territorial dispute with India but rather the evidence of India's antagonism toward their state.[51] India's refusal to grant freedom of self-determination to Muslim Kashmir is part of an attempt to undermine the very idea of their state regarding the establishment of a Muslim national home. According to Muhammad Ayub Khan, the Indian occupation of Kashmir was an expression of the Muslims oppression:

> The Muslims of Kashmir, under Indian control, were no better than hostages. They had no rights, no freedom. Over half a million Muslims had been driven out of India because of the Indian government.[52]

[47] Rizvi, Pakistan's Strategic Culture, 310.

[48] Peter Lavoy (31 October 2016). *Pakistan's Strategic Culture*, U.S. Defense Threat Reduction Agency, 10.

[49] Craig Baxter (2015). Muhammad Ayub Khan, in Roger Long (Ed.), *A History of Pakistan*, Karachi: Oxford University Press, 489.

[50] Hassan Abbas (2005). *Pakistan's Drift into Extremism*, New York: An East Gate Book, 17.

[51] Cohen, *The Idea of Pakistan*, 52.

[52] Altaf Gauhar (1996). *Ayub Khan: Pakistan's First Military Ruler*, Karachi: Oxford University Press, 187.

Such narratives stand out from the statements of Pakistan's leaders over the generations.[53] Even in the last year during the crisis over the repeal by New Delhi of Article 370 of the Indian constitution granting special status to Kashmir, Pakistani decision-makers and military firmly responded. On August 6, 2019, Pakistani Army Chief of Staff, General Qamar Javed Bajwa, stated that the military will "go to any extent" to support Kashmir.[54] Pakistani Prime Minister, Imran Khan, even compared new Indian policy toward Kashmir with Nazi Germany policy in the last century:

> "...the ideology of Hindu supremacy, like the Nazi Aryan supremacy, will not stop" in Kashmir, but would lead to "the suppression of Muslims in India & eventually lead to targeting of Pakistan."[55]

Based on such an image of the enemy, Pakistanis also perceive the geostrategic state of their country through the prism of the Indian enmity. As Zulfikar Ali Bhutto noted, the distribution of territories and India's takeover of areas on Pakistan's eastern border were the reasons for a problematic geostrategic situation:

> These areas were granary of the north and were very important strategically. By giving them to India, the defense of Lahore and other parts of West Pakistan became badly exposed… India's occupation of Junagadh

[53] See for example: Bhutto, *The Myth of Independence*, 173; Sani H. Panhwar (2009). *Benazir Bhutto: Selected Speeches 1989–2007*, 95, http://bhutto.org/Acrobat/BB_Speeches_Book.pdf. Accessed 3 August 2019; Prime Minister Nawaz Sharif (2013–2017): Kashmir Is a Core Dispute Between Pakistan and India (2017, February 2). *Times of India*, http://timesofindia.indiatimes.com/world/pakistan/kashmir-is-core-dispute-between-india-and-pakistan-nawaz-sharif/articleshow/56982014.cms. Accessed 12 August 2019; General Raheel Sharif: Pakistan Will Continue to Support Kashmir on Diplomatic Front (2016, September 7). *Indian Express*, http://indianexpres.com/article/world-news/pakistan-kashmir-dispute. Accessed 12 August 2019.

[54] Asif Shahzad (2019, August 6). Pakistan Army Chief Says Military Will "Go to Any Extent" to Support Kashmir Cause, *Reuters*, https://www.reuters.com/article/us-india-kashmir-pakistan-army/pakistan-army-chief-says-military-will-go-to-any-extent-to-support-kashmir-cause-idUSKCN1UW0ZM. Accessed 12 August 2019.

[55] Rebecca Radcliffe & Shah Meer Baloch (2019, August 11). Imran Khan Likens Inaction Over Kashmir to Appeasing Hitler, *The Guardian*, https://www.theguardian.com/world/2019/aug/11/imran-khan-likens-global-inaction-on-kashmir-to-appeasing-hitler. Accessed 12 August 2019.

and Hyderabad created political and psychological conditions which were of incalculable advantage to her.[56]

To summarize it, Pakistan's strategic culture contains isolationist national self-image. Such an image is based on the antagonism of Muslim entity *vis-à-vis* Hindu one. This antagonism contributed to the image of India as a powerful enemy, with the expansionist aspiration toward the Muslim country. Derived from the rivalry, Pakistani strategic culture also includes the revisionist beliefs of injustice in relation to Kashmir.

In the next pages I will elaborate on the patterns of warfighting of Pakistan as are derived from the threat perception.

The Threat Perception and Warfighting Pattern of the Pakistani Army

It appears that the antagonism toward the powerful India, on the one hand, and the nonacceptance of Indian stance in Kashmiri dispute, on the other, led to the fact that Islamabad has adopted an offensive pattern of warfighting, including, *inter alia:*

- A tendency to initiate and escalate confrontations;
- The adoption of a two-stage strategy: the stage of the sub-war confrontation—initiating the conflict using guerrilla, semi-military forces; and next, transition to a phase of conventional warfare, involving the participation of the Pakistani regular forces.

Why did Pakistan, however, which is weaker than India, choose to act offensively, initiate and escalate 3 of the 4 conventional wars? Based on an objective assessment of the relative power, Pakistan's behavior—initiating and escalation of offensive actions against the stronger enemy—appears irrational. It should be emphasized that three out of the four India–Pakistan wars commenced following the Pakistani attacks aimed at imposing a solution to the Kashmir problem by force. In order to understand this dynamic, we must look to the context of Pakistani strategic culture in which Kashmir is the central narrative. As aforementioned, the acquisition of control over Kashmir, a region populated by a Muslim majority,

---

[56]Bhutto, *The Myth of Independence*, 177–178.

was critical to Pakistan, which had been constituted around the idea of establishing a separate independent state for the Muslim population of the Indian subcontinent.[57] Accordingly, Kashmir was the main reason for initiating and escalating conflicts by Pakistan. In Pakistan's strategic culture Kashmir's occupation by India was perceived as an expression of Indian aggression toward it, which increased the importance of rectifying the injustice by the attachment of Kashmir to Pakistan.

The strategic culture perceptions of the Pakistani politicians and military regarding the strategic threat posed by the Indian army caused the adoption of the combined use of irregular forces with regular ones. It was the result of understanding that given the Pakistani army inferiority *vis-à-vis* the Indian armed forces, the use of irregular forces at the beginning of hostilities could be effective.[58] Since its declaration of independence in 1947, Pakistan has relied on militias as a tool for achieving goals.[59] As will be discussed in Chapter 5, this warfighting pattern was already evident during the first Indo-Pak war. The use of unidentified, semi-military forces at the beginning of a conflict was the result of operational planning by Pakistani military officers, pursuant to which it was enough to resolve a conflict without the assistance of regular forces. By using irregular forces, secretly penetrating the Indian territory, Pakistan's army tried to get an advantage over a more powerful adversary. The use of regular military forces was only a coercion as a result of the failure of irregular forces in the face of Indian military units.

As a weaker side in the conflict with India, Pakistani decision-makers perceived nuclear weaponization as a change of relative power, which grants certain benefits against the stronger enemy. While the images regarding national self-image, image of India's enemy, and geostrategic situation remained stable over decades, a change of relative power perception allowed the Pakistanis to maintain their traditional, pre-nuclear pattern of conventional warfighting. In other words, Pakistan's case study represents a nuclear weaponization influence model of *"Aggression Encouragement."*

---

[57] Sumit Ganguli (1986). *The Origins of War in South Asia: Indo-Pakistani Conflicts Since 1947*, Boulder and London: Westview Press, 45.

[58] Bhashyam Kasturi (2008). The State of War with Pakistan, in Daniel Martson & Chandar Sundaram (Eds.), *A Military History of India and South Asia*, Bloomington and Indianapolis: Indiana University Press, 143.

[59] Seth Jones & Christine Fair (2010). *Counterinsurgency in Pakistan*, Santa Monica: RAND, 7.

While initiating military moves to try to resolve the Kashmir issue by force, nuclear weapons acquisition was perceived as a shield against a retaliation threat of the Indian superior armed forces. The researcher Vipin Narang in reference to Pakistan's nuclear strategy, noted:

> [Islamabad] adopted an asymmetric escalation posture that attempts to credibly deter conventional attack by threatening the first use of nuclear weapon against a large-scale Indian conventional thrust through Pakistan's vulnerable dessert and plains corridor in Sindh and Punjab.[60]

Such assumption can rely on the statement of the former Prime Minister Benazir Bhutto:

> Islamabad saw its [nuclear] capability as a deterrence to any future war with India... India could not have launched a conventional war, because if it did, it would have meant suicide.[61]

As shall be demonstrated below, the change in the relative power perception was already evident given the conduct of the Pakistan army in the course of the Kargil war in 1999: initiation of the confrontation and use of disguised soldiers as irregular forces before using the regular army units. In course of the hostilities, the then Foreign Minister of Pakistan Shamshad Ahmad, issued a clear nuclear threat to deter Indian possible retaliation:

> [Pakistan] will not hesitate to use any weapon in [its] arsenal to defend [its] territorial integrity.[62]

INDIA

Geostrategic Situation

India's geostrategic situation is fundamentally different from that of Pakistan. Unlike its neighbor which suffers from a lack of strategic depth, India is a large country. It is the seventh largest country in the world,

---

[60] Narang, *Nuclear Strategy in the Modern Era*, 57.

[61] Paul Kapur (Fall 2008). Ten Years of Instability in a Nuclear South Asia, *International Security*, 33/2, 75.

[62] Cited in Usman Ghani (September 2012). Nuclear Weapons in India-Pakistan Crisis, *IPRI Journal*, 2, 141–142.

with an area of 3.2 million square kilometers.[63] Similarly to the Pakistan case, the geographical dimension has significantly influenced the country's security.[64]

The country shares its border with several countries: Pakistan, China, Nepal, Bhutan, Myanmar, and Bangladesh. After the declaration of independence by India, Pakistan became New Delhi's main threat.[65] The length of the border with Pakistan is 3323 km.[66] Additionally, India and Pakistan share a 776-km common border in the Kashmiri region, the Line of Control (LoC), which is in fact the cease-fire line.[67] Compared to Pakistan, India's territory is four times larger, which undoubtedly gives New Delhi an advantage in terms of territorial depth.[68] In addition to this geographical advantage, India also has a distinct advantage over Islamabad in terms of conventional military power.[69] As shall be demonstrated below, these figures undoubtedly affected India's military preparedness for the Pakistani threat.

As abovementioned, until 1971 Pakistan was divided into two parts, eastern and western, which posed for the Indian Army a threat of a potential scenario of fighting on two fronts simultaneously. Thus, for instance, during the tension between the two states in February and March 1950, the Indian army deployed its units both near the borders with western and eastern parts of the Muslim country.[70] After 1971, upon the establishment of the independent state of Bangladesh state, there has been some improvement in India's geostrategic situation, mainly removing the threat of war on the two fronts.[71]

[63] Harjeet Singh (2009). *India's strategic Culture: The Impact of Geography*, New Delhi: Center for Land Warfare Studies, 3.

[64] George Tanham (1992). *Indian Strategic Thought*, Santa Monica: RAND, 2.

[65] Lt Gen. (Ret.) A. Hasnan Habib (1992). An Indonesian View of India's Strategic Development, in Ross Babbage & Sandy Gordon (Eds.), *India's Strategic Future*, Oxford: Oxford University Press, 114.

[66] Pushita Das (2010). Introduction, in Pushita Das (Ed.), *India's Border Management: Selected Documents*, New Delhi: Institute for Defense studies and Analysis, 1.

[67] Das, Introduction, 10.

[68] Walter Ludwig (Winter 2007/2008). A Cold Start for Hot Wars? *International Security*, 32/3, 174.

[69] Narang, *Nuclear Strategy in the Modern Era*, 109.

[70] Lorne Kavic (1967). *India's Quest for Security: Defense Policies, 1947–1965*, Berkeley and Los Angeles: University of California Press, 84.

[71] Ganti Sury Bhargava (1976). *India's Security in the 1980s*, London: The International Center for Strategic Studies, 10.

Since 1962, China has also become India's rival. The Chinese challenge over time has also been reflected in the strategic cooperation of Beijing and Pakistan, which again brought back the threat of war on two fronts.[72] The territorial conflict with China was around the border with Tibet.[73] With the Chinese invasion of Tibet and the annexation of this territory in 1950, seeds of controversy and future war between the two countries were sown, as the Chinese never acknowledged legitimacy of the existing borderline. In terms of India's geostrategy, the annexation of Tibet by China eliminated territorial buffer, protecting India from the Chinese army.[74] In 1962, a border war broke out between the two countries.[75] Following the Indian defeat in the war, China occupied parts of the Kashmir region.

It should be emphasized, however, that the level of tension with China and the frequency of military conflicts with its military are not the same as with Pakistan. Except for a month-long war in 1962 that, India has not had to fight with the Chinese ever since. Therefore, for the purpose of examining warfighting patterns of the Indian military, the balance of power between these two countries is relatively less important. This of course is opposite to the relations with Pakistan, also highlighted in the Indian strategic culture.

Size of Indian Military

Following the partition of British India, the size of independent India's military reached 280,000 soldiers.[76] As early as 1947, the guideline for determining the size of the Indian army was the level of threat posed to the country. According to India's first Secretary of Defense, Bhalja:

> In present world conditions security can only be guaranteed by the maintenance of sufficient armed forces to encourage friends and deter possible aggressors, thus ensuring from all a healthy and friendly respect.[77]

---

[72]Tanham, *Indian Strategic Thought*, 36.

[73]Commodore Katherine Richards (February 2015). *China-India: An Analysis of the Himalayan Territorial Dispute*, Australian Defense College, Center for Defense and Strategic Studies, 4.

[74]Richards, *China-India*, 8.

[75]R. Sukumaram (July–September 2003). The 1962 India-China War and Kargil 1999: Restrictions of the Use of Air Power, *Strategic Analysis*, 27/3, 332.

[76]Kavic, India's Quest for Security, 82.

[77]Kavic, India's Quest for Security, 29.

Fig. 4.3 Indian military (thousands) (*Source* World Military Expenditures and Arms Transfers, http://www.state.gov/t/avc/rls/rpt/wmeat. Accessed 29 August 2019)

Overall, since 1947 the number of the Indian armed forces has grown steadily and this trend has been supported by parallel dynamics of the accelerated growth rate of the country's population. According to World Bank Data, India's population has grown steadily, reaching in 2018 1353 billion people.[78]

Eventually, this dynamic granted to India's military a definite quantitative advantage over the Pakistani armed forces. As aforementioned, with regard to the Pakistani military, quantitative asymmetry has been maintained for decades over an average of 1–2 in favor of India. According to the data below (see Fig. 4.3) till 1980 the India's military personnel has increased. It could be assumed that in accordance with the Pakistani case study, this steady increase in military personnel was due to the repeated large-scale armed conflicts between both countries. In 1980, this trend changed and the size of the army decreased until the mid-1990s when New Delhi began to increase the quantity of its military personnel again. Nevertheless, unlike the Pakistan military, the Indian army did not cross again the peak of 1975. As of 2016, the Indian

[78] See: India Population, World Bank, https://data.worldbank.org/indicator/SP.POP. TOTL?locations=IN&view=chart. Accessed 18 November 2019.

military numbering over 1.4 million was twice the size of the Pakistan Army, with its 615,000 soldiers. Additionally, India's armed forces have also a qualitative advantage over the Pakistani military.[79]

Practically speaking, given such asymmetry, the India's ability to allocate more men and resources to the fighting grants it an advantage over Pakistani armed forces in a prolonged conventional engagement.[80]

India's Military Budget

Upon the end of the British mandate, India inherited one of the world's failing economies.[81] This problematic starting point, however, has been further translated into significant economic growth, making India one of the world's most important economies. The growth in the state's economy has also allowed an increase in military expenditure (see Fig. 4.4).

As in the case of Pakistan, the growth of India's defense budget has also been affected by the threats against it. One can identify sharp increases in defense budget scope following the wars waged by India: in 1965, after the war with China and the second war with Pakistan the defense budget increased from 0.682 billion dollars to the level of 2.162 billion USD. After a slight decrease in the defense expenditure in 1970 (1.833 billion USD), since 1975, four years after the third Indo-Pak war the budget begun steadily to increase.

Furthermore, compared to Pakistan, India's stronger economy and fast economic growth allowed it to allocate more resources to the military budget.[82]

In view of the foregoing, India's relative advantage over its rival Pakistan is not associated merely with military expenditure. Compared to Islamabad, New Delhi does not suffer from strategic depth problem and even benefits from quantitative superiority over Pakistani military. In other words, India's relative material power is greater than Pakistan's.

[79] Khan, *Eating Grass*, 216.

[80] Francisco Aguilar, Randy Bell, Natalie Black, et al. (2011). *An Introduction to Pakistan's Military*, Cambridge: Belfer Center for Science and International Affairs, 10.

[81] Hasmot Ali (June 2016). Economic Change in India Since Independence (1947–1965), *IRJIMS*, 2/4, 47.

[82] Shane Mason (2016). *Military Budgets in India and Pakistan: Trajectories, Priorities and Risks*, Washington, DC: Stimson Center, 36.

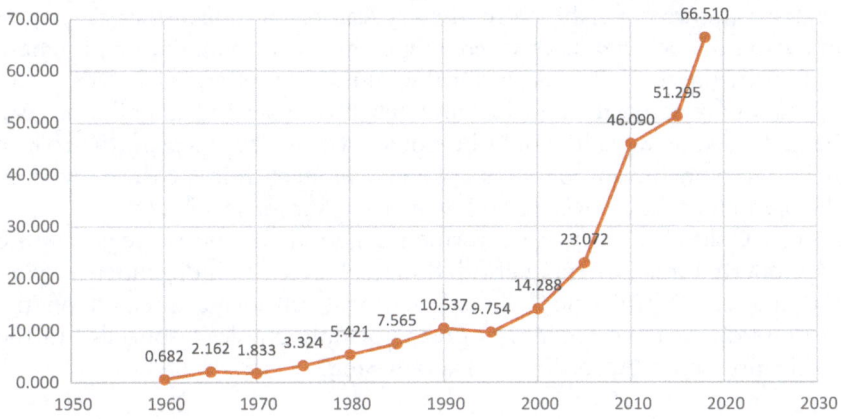

Fig. 4.4 India's military expenditure, billions (USD) (*Source* World Bank Data, https://data.worldbank.org/indicator/MS.MIL.XPND.CD. Accessed 26 November 2019)

Strategic Culture

The review of India's strategic culture sets a certain challenge: lack of literature on strategic issues, in general and on strategic culture, in particular. Jaswant Singh attributes this lack to many historical and religious reasons.[83] As the scholar George Tanham noted:

> India does not admit easily to broad generalizations. It is extraordinary complex and diverse society, and Indian elites show little evidence of having thought coherently and systematically about national strategy... The lacunae and ambiguities seem compatible with a culture that encompasses and accommodates readily to complexity and contradiction.[84]

Exceptions in this regard are the essays and speeches of India's first Prime Minister, Jawaharlal Nehru, who has been heavily involved in defense issues and whose perceptions and attitude influenced Indian

[83] Jaswant Sing (1999). *Defending India*, Bangalore: Macmillan India Ltd., 16.
[84] Tanham, *Indian Strategic Thought*, 5.

strategic culture.[85] Furthermore, the key features of Indian strategic culture in respect of nuclear weapons were shaped mainly by him, during his tenure as Prime Minister.[86] Beyond it, for the purposes of review of India's strategic culture concept, the attitudes and beliefs of other Indian politicians will be addressed as well. It should be noted that, unlike Pakistan, the role of the military in Indian politics is extremely limited, as it is characterized by the predominance of civilians and politicians over military.[87]

The Cold War years are a formative period for the strategic culture of modern India. In this period India achieved its independence from the colonial British rule.[88] India's national self-image is based on the assumption that the country is great not only physically but also in the civilization sense. According to Jaswant Sing:

> To mind comes an ancient truism about two of the great civilizations of Asia, Indian and Chinese, that India has always existed without a state, but that China cannot exist without one.[89]

Pursuant to such perception, the desire to be one of the strongest powers in the world is a central narrative of India's foreign policy.[90] The expression of this approach could be found in Nehru's statement:

> We belong to a great country, a country that is not only great physically but in things far more important. If we are to be worthy of our country, we must have big minds and big hearts, for small men cannot face big issues or accomplish big tasks...I have faith in India and her great destiny.[91]

[85] Kanti Bajpai (2002). Indian Strategic Culture, in Michael Chambers (Ed.), *South Asia in 2020: Future Strategic Balances and Alliances*, Carlisle, PA: Strategic Studies Institute, 245.

[86] Rajesh Basrur (March 2001). Nuclear Weapons and Indian Strategic Culture, *Journal of Peace Research*, 38/2, 185.

[87] Stephen Cohen & Sunil Dasgupta (2013). *Arming Without Aiming*, Washington, DC: Brookings Institution Press, 147.

[88] Jerome Conley (2001). *Indo-Russian Military and Nuclear Cooperation*, Lanham, MD: Lexington Books, 87.

[89] Sing, *Defending India*, 10.

[90] Chris Ogden (2014). *Indian Foreign Policy: Ambition and Transition*, Cambridge: Polity Press, 3.

[91] Two Years of Independence (1954). *Jawaharlal Nehru's Speeches, August 1949–February 1953*, New Delhi: Publications Division, 2–6.

From Nehru's point of view, independent modern India is the result of millennial history.[92] Despite the aspiration for global status, India is a status quo state. As the first Indian Prime Minister stated:

> We are not hostile to any country and we do not want to meddle in other people's affairs. Every nation should be free to choose the path it considers best. We do not wish to interfere with the freedom of other nations and we expect them to feel the same about our freedom. We have decided to follow this policy, not only because it is essentially a sound one from our country's point of view but also because it seems to be the only way to serve the cause of world peace.[93]

A similar position was also expressed by Prime Minister Indira Gandhi, Nehru's daughter. In her speech in Parliament on February 27, 1973, she declared:

> We in government of India don't believe in power politics. We don't desire the status or perquisites of what is as conventional power… this kind of thinking by anybody that he is dominant or that a big power has some kind of divine right to a sphere of influence, just does not apply in the contemporary world.[94]

This status quo policy, however, does not appear to be a compromising and conciliatory policy: the key characteristic of Indian strategic culture is an aggressive and assertive position toward any outside attempt to undermine its territorial integrity or harm to its interests. As an independent and young country, India has developed considerable sensitivity to threats to its territorial integrity.[95] Indian strategic culture recognizes that interests, power, and even violence are a central part of international relations. Conflict and war are not an uncommon phenomenon in the international arena.[96] Nehru had no doubts regarding the necessity of military force to ensure the survival of the state:

---

[92] Yaacov Verzberger (1984). *Misperceptions in Foreign Policymaking: The Sino-Indian Conflict, 1959–1962*, Boulder: Westview Press, 205.

[93] Two Years of Independence, 4.

[94] Strength and Maturity (1984). *Selected Speeches and Writings of Indira Gandhi, September 1972–March 1977*, New Delhi: Publications Division, 14.

[95] Verzberger, *Misperceptions in Foreign Policymaking*, 206.

[96] Bajpai, Indian Strategic Culture, 250.

Although every intelligent person must realize that a war must be avoided at all costs, no country can do away with the apparatus of war. At least, no responsible government dare takes that step. If we value our freedom, we cannot afford to depend only on the good in human nature because we live in a harsh and cruel world. We have to depend on our own strength and be prepared to defend our freedom.[97]

Similarly, Mahatma Gandhi, who opposed violence and even adopted nonviolent opposition to colonial rule, argued that it is necessary to use crude force to maintain India's independence:

I would rather have India resort to arms in order to defend her honor than that she should, in a cowardly manner, become or remain a helpless victim of her dishonor.[98]

The Indo-Pak wars over Kashmir are an example of such an attitude. The struggle for Kashmir is perceived as a test of the state's ability to secure its territorial sovereignty and to protect citizens.[99] The Prime Minister Nehru, referring to the Kashmir issue, noted:

Well, we have tried to fashion our actions in regard to this problem according to what we considered to be our obligations and responsibilities...The first was to protect and safeguard the territory of India from every invasion. That is the primary responsibility of the State. Secondly, it was our duty to honor the pledge we gave to the people of Jammu and Kashmir State. And that pledge was a two-fold pledge. We were obliged to protect them from invasion and rape and loot and arson and everything that accompanied that invasion. That was the first part of the pledge. The second part of the pledge was given by us unilaterally and was to the effect that it would be for the people to decide finally what their future was to be.[100]

The Kashmir issue has not lost its importance in the Indian strategic culture over the years. In 1994 Prime Minister Narasimha Rao in his

---

[97] India is Opposed to War (1954). *Jawaharlal Nehru's Speeches, August 1949–February 1953*, New Delhi: Publications Division, 183.

[98] Lawrence Sondhause (2006). *Strategic Culture and Ways of War*, Abingdon, Oxon: Routledge, 94.

[99] Ogden, *Indian Foreign Policy*, 67.

[100] Let the People to Decide, (1954). Jawaharlal Nehru's Speeches, *August 1949–February 1953*, New Delhi: Publications Division, 101.

Independence Day speech addressed Islamabad and said that it should return to India the occupied part of Kashmir.[101] Recently, the Prime Minister Narendra Modi, in his speech devoted to the cancelation of the relevant constitution's article granting special status to Kashmir, reiterated the attitude that this area is an integral part of India and stressed the negative role Pakistan plays in the region.[102]

As part of the enemy image, Pakistan is perceived in the Indian strategic culture as an aggressive country. In this respect India's first Prime Minister noted:

...there has been a continuous and intensive propaganda in Pakistan for jehad against India. Above all, India desires peace for herself and peace in the world. Let me, however, remind everyone concerned, that India is not quite so weak or helpless that she should submit to insults and the threats of jehad.[103]

Such assumption also appeared in Indira Gandhi's statement:

...in spite of grave provocation, we have never interfered in what has happening on the other side... In 1965 how did the war start? We did not start it. It started because thousands of infiltrators were sent into Kashmir thinking... that the people of Kashmir were not with India and therefore if people came from Pakistan the local people would help them... Pakistan is trying to do the same thing this time.[104]

These attitudes and assumptions of Indian politicians emphasized the contrast between New Delhi's status quo policy and Islamabad's

[101] A Look at the Independence Day Speeches Made by Prime Ministers Since 1991 (2018, August 15). *Hindustan Times*, https://m.hindustantimes.com/india-news/a-look-at-the-independence-day-speeches-made-by-prime-ministers-since-1991/story-W06QQX-6jlT9mAQAn8Dk9HI_amp.html. Accessed 26 August 2019.

[102] Narendra Modi Speech (2019, August 8). https://www.narendramodi.in/prime-minister-narendra-modi-s-address-to-the-nation-on-8th-august-2019-545901. Accessed 26 August 2019

[103] We Will Not Compromise (1954). *Jawaharlal Nehru's Speeches, August 1949–February 1953*, New Delhi: Publications Division, 292–293.

[104] Indira Ghandi (1972). *India and Bangla Desh: Selected Speeches and Statements, March to December 1971*, New Delhi: Orient Longman Limited, 77–78.

aggressive behavior. It is not surprising that as a result of such beliefs, perceptions regarding geostrategic situation were also shaped through the prism of the Pakistani threat.[105]

The Threat Perception and Warfighting Pattern of the Indian Army

Based on such strategic culture perceptions, the Indian military adopted a defensive, restrained warfighting pattern as follows:

- Non-initiation of wars and reacting to aggression;
- A tendency to escalate a conflict after the start of hostilities, mainly by expanding the geographic scope of the combat zone, including transferring the war to enemy's territory.

These features are in line with the country's strategic culture. Given the material power asymmetry in favor of India, the Indian politicians didn't perceive Pakistan as an existential threat that would justify taking offensive strategies to prevent the threat. The national self-image of great and powerful India, superior to artificially created Pakistan resulted in the adoption of a defensive pattern of warfighting. None of the Indo-Pak wars broke out as a result of New Delhi's initiative. India reacted to aggressive action of Pakistan. Nevertheless, following India's sensibility to threats against its territorial integrity or interests, is embedded in the country's strategic culture the readiness to aggressively act against such threats. Indeed, in the course of the fighting against Pakistani invasions in the pre-weaponization period Indian military didn't hesitate to escalate the conflict by transferring the war to the Pakistani territory.

Regarding the nuclear weaponization, India reflects a different model of weaponization influence on warfighting patterns. Like Pakistanis, Indian decision-makers perceived nuclear weaponization as a change of relative power. This change, however, in relative power was perceived differently by decision-makers in New Delhi—India changed its preference of conventional warfighting pattern. The nuclear weapons possession by Pakistan, the country which perceived through strategic culture lens as revisionist, aggressive enemy, caused to restraint on the Indian military in the battlefield. Namely, India represents the

---

[105] See for example: *Selected Works of Jawaharlal Nehru, 26 October 1950–28 February 1951* (1993). New Delhi: Jawaharlal Nehru Memorial Fund, 344–345.

nuclear weaponization model of *Restraint Imposition*. Following the
change in relative power perception, Indian military changed the preference of pattern of conventional warfighting. On the one hand, as previously in the pre-weaponization period India had not initiated the war
but only reacted to the invasion of Pakistanis, in correspondence with
the first characteristic of the Indian warfighting pattern. On the other
hand, India refrained from expanding the confrontation and transferring the fighting to the enemy's territory. According to the logic of the
"Weak-Strong Actors Paradox," India as a stronger side in the conflict
is restrained escalating to the full-scale conventional offensive, including
expanding a geographical scope of war, due to the fear from deterioration to nuclear war with Pakistan, which as a weaker side could respond
using its nonconventional arsenal.

This India's military restraint was already evident during the 1999
Kargil war. As the researchers Ganguli and Hagerty noted:

> In effect, the mutual possession of nuclear weapons was the critical deter-
> minant in controlling both vertical and horizontal escalation. The Indian
> politico-military elite was now acutely cognizant of Pakistan's status as an
> overt nuclear weapons state, and therefore realized it would act with con-
> siderable restraint.[106]

According to the Indian Army Chief of Staff during Kargil war, General
Malik, the Indian Prime Minister requested the army to refrain from
crossing the international border with Pakistan:

> The next day, 25 May 1999, Prime Minister Vajpayee declared that the
> new situation was not infiltration but a move to occupy Indian territory.
> He said that "all steps will be taken to clear the Kargil area." He also
> declared that Indian troops would not cross the LoC.[107]

General Malik also emphasized that nuclear weapons played a role in the
considerations of decision-makers:

[106] Sumit Ganguli & Devin Hagerty (2005). *Fearful Symmetry: India-Pakistan Crises in the Shadow of Nuclear Weapons*, Seattle: University of Washington Press, 161.

[107] General V. P. Malik (2016). *India's Military Conflicts and Diplomacy*, New Delhi: HarperCollins Publishers India, 252.

...the nuclear factor played on the minds of the political decision makers. It posted little problems for a limited war. But political and military planning for conflict escalation had to be carried carefully. Escalation control was essential.[108]

ISRAEL

Geostrategic Situation

Israel is deemed to represent a classic case of a state whose military doctrine was affected by geographical considerations, e.g., territorial asymmetry *vis-à-vis* hostile Arab countries, long borders, and lack of strategic depth.[109] These conditions constituted one of Israel's most important strategic constraints. Indeed, during the Independence War (1948–1949) Israel expanded its territory as compared to that planned for the Jewish state in the UN resolution of 1947. The boundaries created, however, were problematic in terms of defense ability. The territorial asymmetry among Israel and the Arab states was significant: the total territory of Arab countries bordering Israel (Syria, Jordan, Egypt, and Lebanon) was approximately 58 times larger than the territory of Israel.[110] Due to such a situation almost every point in Israel was threatened by the neighboring Arab countries. There was also a disproportion between the total length of the borders and the territory of the state of Israel.[111]

In the east, the Jordanian army took control of Judea and Samaria territory, posing an immediate threat to central Israel and population concentrations in the region were subject to the threat of Jordanian artillery. To the northeast, Syrian control of the Golan Heights created

---

[108] General V. P. Malik (2006). *Kargil: From Surprise to Victory*, New Delhi: HarperCollins Publishers India, 253.

[109] Michael Handel (1994). The Evolution of Israeli Strategy: The Psychology of Insecurity and the Quest for Absolute Security, in Williamson Murray, Macgregor Knox, & Alvin Bernstein (Eds.), *The Making of Strategy*, New York: Cambridge University Press, 535.

[110] Avner Yaniv (1994). *Politics and Strategy in Israel*, Tel Aviv: Sifriyat Poalim, 16 [in Hebrew].

[111] Avner Simchoni (2006). *Strategic Depth and the Eastern Front*, Tel Aviv: Tel Aviv University, 13 [in Hebrew].

a permanent threat to the Hula Valley and Galilee settlements. On the northern border of the state of Israel, a threat also developed from Lebanon. As for the southern border, the occupation of the Gaza Strip and the concentration of the Egyptian units in the Sinai Peninsula created a constant threat to the southern part of the country.

Until the Six-Day War (1967), Israel was particularly sensitive to the problem of depth. The lack of strategic depth caused a serious danger to the state and thus it was exposed to an additional form of territorial asymmetry *vis-à-vis* Arab countries, which have large territories.[112] On the one hand, a lack of strategic depth created a problem of reducing the operative maneuvering space of Israeli forces, due to the proximity of the country's vital centers to the border. On the other hand, a narrow area created a problem of absorbing an attack, especially a surprise attack, even before sufficient military force was put in place to repel it.[113] The significance of the Israeli geostrategic situation, expressed in the absence of strategic depth, is that the enemy's tactical capabilities (such as small arms and artillery fire) posed a strategic threat to it.[114] Major cities such as Jerusalem were within the range of the enemy artillery. Airports were within a 3–5-minute flight range of Syrian and Jordanian air forces.[115] It should be noted that despite the territorial achievements of the Six-Day war, Israel's geostrategic situation has not changed. Although a kind of strategic depth was gained by Israel through the control of the Sinai, the Golan Heights, and the West Bank, new settlements which were established near the new border, limited the Israeli army freedom of action.[116]

Nevertheless, the peace treaties executed with Egypt on March 26, 1976, and with Jordan on October 26, 1994, significantly affected Israel's geostrategic situation. Although these agreements did not

[112]Ariel Levita (1988). *The Military Doctrine of Israel: Defense and Attack*, Tel Aviv: Hakibbutz Hameuhad, 30 [in Hebrew].

[113]Dan Horowitz (1985). The Permanent and Changing Concept of Israeli Security, in Aharon Yariv & Yosef Alper (Eds.), *War of Choice*, Tel Aviv: Hakibbutz Hameuhad, 68–69 [in Hebrew].

[114]Ron Tira (September 2008). *The Struggle for the Nature of War*, Tel Aviv: National Security Research Institute, 28.

[115]Handel, The Evolution of Israeli Strategy, 537.

[116]Avi Kober (1995). *Military Decision in Israeli-Arabs Wars 1948–1982*, Tel Aviv: Maarachot, 149 [in Hebrew].

improve Israel's geographical conditions, and Sinai Peninsula was returned to Egypt, the end of the conflict with two Arab countries, and especially with a powerful country such as Egypt, reduced Israel's fear of a combined attack of Arab coalition.

Size of the Israeli Military

For decades, due to natural growth and immigration to the Jewish state, the size of the Israeli army has increased (see Fig. 4.5). Nevertheless, since its independence, the population of Israel was significantly smaller than the population of any neighboring Arab state and certainly compared to the Arab world as a whole. As a result, Israel faces the quantitative inferiority *vis-à-vis* its Arab enemies.[117] The quantitative inferiority exists even when all the Israeli armed forces, including the reserve forces, are mobilized. Over the years, the quantitative asymmetry between Israel and Egypt, Jordan, Syria, and Iraq has increased: from a 1:2 ratio in favor of the Arab states in the Six-Day War the situation has deteriorated to about 1:3 ratio in the Yom Kippur War, and has continued to decline to 1:5 ratio in 1989.[118]

Although during the Independence War, the balance of forces in terms of the forces engaged in the fighting was in favor of the Israeli army,[119] the Israeli military preparedness was influenced by the fact that Israel has a significant quantitative inferiority *vis-à-vis* the Arabs in natural resources and population.[120] The necessity of waging most wars (except Sinai in 1956) on more than one front simultaneously, exacerbated the problem of the Israeli quantitative asymmetry. Thus, for instance, during the Six-Day War, the Israeli military fought on three fronts: on the southern front against the Egyptian army, on the eastern front against the Jordanian army, and on the northeastern one against the Syrian army. This forced Israelis to divide their forces on several fronts, which further worsened the quantitative asymmetry of Israel

---

[117] Israel Tal (1996). *National Security: Few vs. Many*, Tel Aviv: Dvir, 50 [in Hebrew].

[118] Kober, *Military Decision in Israeli-Arabs Wars 1948–1982*, 148.

[119] Zeev Maoz (2009). *Defending the Holy Land*, Ann Arbor: The University of Michigan Press, 4.

[120] Avraham Rotem (2002). A Smart Small Army—Vision or Legend?, in Haggai Golan (Ed.), *Israel's Security Web: Core Issues of Israel's National Security in its Sixth Decade*, Tel Aviv: Maarahot, 75 [in Hebrew].

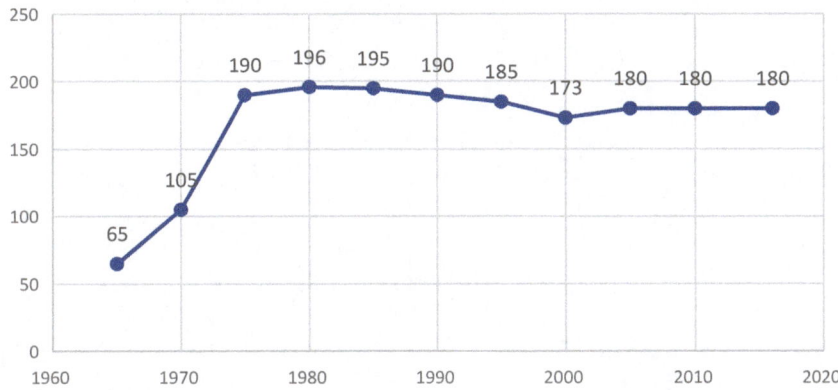

Fig. 4.5 Israeli military (thousands) (*Source* World Military Expenditures and Arms Transfers, http://www.state.gov/t/avc/rls/rpt/wmeat. Accessed 29 August 2019)

vis-à-vis the enemies' armies, which also gained reinforcements from other Arab countries.[121]

Consequently, in terms of relative power balance, Israel with restricted resources and a small population, that the majority thereof is recruited during a wartime, is unable to conduct a prolonged war. Mobilization of forces for a long time had the potential to damage the country's economy. As we will see below, the perception of such asymmetry has influenced the pattern of the Israeli warfighting.

Israel's Military Budget

Over the years, Israel has invested heavily in security (see Fig. 4.6). The significant military expenditure was required to balance the clear quantitative advantage of Arab countries by gaining a qualitative advantage—a key component of Israeli security doctrine.[122] Israel understood that it

[121] Kober, *Military Decision in Israeli-Arabs Wars 1948–1982*, 150.
[122] Handel, The Evolution of Israeli Strategy, 546.

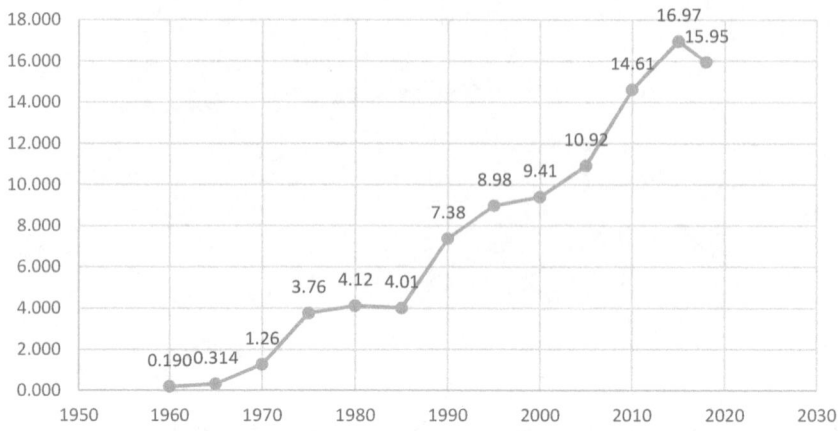

Fig. 4.6 Israel's military expenditure, billions (USD) (*Source* World Bank Data, https://data.worldbank.org/indicator/MS.MIL.XPND.CD. Accessed 26 November 2019)

could not compete with the Arabs on the quantitative level, and thus "transferred" the race to the qualitative field. This was reflected in efforts to produce or obtain advanced weapon systems, mainly from Western suppliers. In accordance with this policy, Israel's defense budget grows on average by 260% each decade.

External assistance and weapons acquisition in the 1950s and 1960s from France, and since the late 1960s from the United States and Western Germany played an important role in efforts to sustain Israeli qualitative advantage. Washington is considered the main Israeli's ally providing it with most sophisticated weapons. The goal of the US commitment toward Israeli security is "to maintain Israel's 'qualitative military edge' (QME) over neighboring militaries."[123] In 2012 the US Congress passed the United States-Israel Enhanced Security Cooperation Act. Pursuant to the provisions of such an act, the United States is committed "to help the Government of Israel to preserve its qualitative military edge amid rapid and uncertain regional political transformation."

[123] U.S. Foreign Aid to Israel (2019, August 7), Congressional Research Service, 2, https://fas.org/sgp/crs/mideast/RL33222.pdf. Accessed 27 November 2019.

At the same time, the US government as the main supplier of weapons and military equipment, *inter alia*, to the Arab Gulf States, has to balance between its defense commitments toward those countries and its legal commitment to preserve Israeli QME.[124]

In view of the foregoing, despite the growing military budgets, Israel has failed to reach resources symmetry *vis-à-vis* Arab countries. On the contrary, the analysis of the geostrategic situation, the size of the military and the resources indicates the advantage of the neighboring Arab countries in terms of relative material power.

We will examine below how this objective power asymmetry is expressed in the perceptions and the approaches of the Israeli decision-makers regarding the strategic threat posed by the neighboring Arab countries.

Strategic Culture

The conventional threat of Arab armies, and the abovementioned security problems associated with it, are reflected in the Israeli strategic culture. It is reflected, first of all, in the essays and statements of Israel's first Prime Minister David Ben-Gurion, whose attitudes and views, along with attitudes of other politicians, significantly influenced Israeli strategic culture. The foundations of the Israeli military doctrine were laid down by Ben-Gurion in the early years of independent Israel. Moreover, its ideas are accepted by the security community and seen at present.[125]

It should be noted that unlike the Indian case study, due to the centrality of the defense issues and significant role the army plays in Israeli society, the Israeli strategic culture is also significantly shaped by the perceptions and attitudes of military officers (besides the politicians).

The strategic culture is predicated on a self-perception of the country as a national home for the Jewish people, which had suffered persecution and danger for centuries. With the attainment of political sovereignty, and given a relative power asymmetry in favor of Arab adversaries, the historical experience of victimhood has evolved into a "siege mentality": a fundamental component of Israel's strategic culture.[126]

---

[124] U.S. Foreign Aid to Israel (2019, August 7). Congressional Research Service, 3–4.

[125] Maoz, *Defending the Holy Land*, 7.

[126] Dmitri Adamsky (2012). *Strategic Culture and Military Innovation*, Ben Shemen: Modan Publishing, 109 [in Hebrew].

The problematic strategic conditions that have prevailed since the achievement of independence in 1948 have only exacerbated this sense of siege.

According to the scholar Zeev Maoz, one of the existing assumptions defining the threat perception by Israeli decision-makers is the Israeli power asymmetry *vis-à-vis* Arab world:

> No matter how widely or how narrowly we define the boundaries of the Arab world, Israel faces enemies that are much more populous, have vastly larger territory, possess more natural resources, and are better networked with the outside world that Israel. Even if these resources are not spent directly on the mission of destroying Israel, the pool of resources at the disposal of Arab leaders creates a threat of vast magnitude.[127]

Consequently, a dominant narrative in the Israeli strategic culture is the quantitative inferiority *vis-à-vis* hostile Arab states, or, in other words, a self-image of "few versus many". This concept has become integral to Israel's military doctrine. According to Ben-Gurion:

> We have a unique military problem - we are few and our enemies are numerous …if wars are expected in the future - and no one can say that they are not expected - then we will face this situation, even if our country's population will increase, and it increases, it increases. But even if it is multiplied and tripled and squared - we will have to face as a few versus many, because there is no objective possibility that we will ever compare our number to the actual and potential enemy in the future. And the number you know - is a big factor in the military, usually a crucial factor.[128]

On another occasion, the first Prime Minister noted:

> A permanent physical fact in our history, and results in many phenomena in our history these days and times: we have always been and remain a small nation to this day. This mathematic has many consequences in our destiny…[129]

[127] Maoz, *Defending the Holy Land*, 8.
[128] David Ben-Gurion (1971). *Yiud i-Yihud*, Tel Aviv: Maarahot, 43 [in Hebrew].
[129] Ben-Gurion, *Yiud i-Yihud*, 110.

General Yigal Alon, who later became a senior politician, noted that the quantitative asymmetry between Israel and the Arab states is so severe that even a population increase will not radically change the situation:

> Israel's quantitative inferiority is a given fact. Even if all Jews around the world would come to Israel, the enemy still would have had a large quantitative advantage... This severe inferiority must have given rise to the concern of the people of Israel and its government and requires attention and action.[130]

Another example of this attitude can be found, for example, in the reference of the military intelligence chief during the Yom Kippur War, General Eli Zeira.[131]

In view of the threat posed by Arab countries, the dominant perception of its Arab enemies is one of total and uncompromising hostility toward the very existence of the Jewish state. According to Ben-Gurion:

> Each country has its own security problem, and there may be contradictions and disputes among different countries regarding foreign or domestic relations... The State of Israel is not free from these problems. But the essence of our security problem is our very existence, our existence as a state and our existence as human beings.[132]

General Israel Tal also emphasized in his book the cause of antisemitism as the source of Arab hostility to the Jewish state:

> ...sometimes in Western countries, also anti-Semitic background contributes to taking anti- Israeli positions. Whereas in Asia and Africa, whose cultures do not derive from Christian heritage, there is the opposite phenomenon: anti-Israeli interests may give rise to anti-Semitic attitudes.[133]

Even over decades, this perception continued to dominate. For example, in his speech on April 23, 2017, at the Holocaust Remembrance Day

---

[130] Yigal Alon (1968). *Masah shel Hol*, Tel Aviv: United Kibbutz Publishing, 36 [in Hebrew].

[131] Eli Zeira (2004). *Myth vs. Reality*, Tel Aviv: Miskal, 41 [in Hebrew].

[132] Ben-Gurion, *Yiud i-Yihud*, 145.

[133] Tal, *National Security*, 48.

ceremony Prime Minister Benjamin Netanyahu noted antisemitism as an expression of Radical Islam enmity toward the Jewish state.[134]

The perception of existential threat even took a concrete form in the Israeli strategic culture. For instance, in view of anti-Israeli rhetoric, Ben-Gurion and the security elite saw in the early 1950s the rise to power in Egypt of a charismatic leader, Gamal Abdel Nasser, as a significant threat.[135]

Regarding the geostrategic situation of the country, prominent is the perception of Israeli politicians and military officers of problematic boundaries in terms of defense capability, which, as discussed in the previous pages, put the country, especially before the Six-Day War in June 1967, under the danger of invasion and occupation without prior warning. Thus, for instance, Ben-Gurion, expressed, in his article, his position on:

> The main center of our country is the Tel Aviv area, which is only 62 kilometers away from the Egyptian border and 21 kilometers from the Jordanian border; Jerusalem lies on the border; Haifa is only 37 kilometers away from the Jordan border; 63 kilometers from the Syrian border. Our enemies can attack us with full force from land, from the sea (Egypt has two destroyers) ... and from the air, and if they arrive to Tel Aviv before we prepare and mobilize our full forces - we are lost.[136]

Yigal Alon referred to this problematic situation also from a military perspective:

> Wide and populous countries can of course in wartime to pursue a strategy of retreat for some time for a future attack ... It is not an Israel's situation. In major wars, any withdrawal would jeopardize the integrity and resilience of the entire country. The Israeli Defense Forces have no place to withdraw. Not a strategic retreat, and in most of the cases not even tactical. No choice but stubborn defense.[137]

---

[134] Premier-Minister Netanyahu's Speech on Holocaust Remembrance Day at Yad Vashem (2017, April 23). http://www.pmo.gov.il/MediaCenter/Speeches/Pages/speechYadVashem230417.aspx. Accessed 5 September 2019 [in Hebrew].

[135] Maoz, *Defending the Holy Land*, 50.

[136] David Ben-Gurion (1981). Military and State, *Maarahot*, 279–280, 6–7 [in Hebrew].

[137] Alon, *Masah shel Hol*, 67.

Accordingly, the loss of territory for Israel endangers its very survival.[138] Despite the territorial achievements of the Six-Day War, the perception of the geostrategic situation didn't change. Thus, General Israel Tal, referring to the borders created in 1967 after the war, described the geostrategic situation of Israel as follows:

> Israel has no strategic depth. It has a small area and in modern warfare it is a more operative than strategic arena – with and without the territories it conquered during the Six Day War. Only when Israel controlled Sinai did it have any real strategic depth in the south… Immediate initial success of an Arab attack could lead to the fall of Israel's vital strategic assets.[139]

It should be emphasized that over the years, even in light of the increasing threat of missiles on Israel, this perception of the Israeli problematic geostrategic situation has remained constant. Thus, in the document titled "The Israeli Defense Forces Strategy" which was published in 2015, updated in April 2018 and seems to reflect the attitudes of the Israeli senior officers, one of the goals of the army during a war is to transfer the hostilities into enemy territory as quickly as possible.[140]

In light of the above, despite technological and geographical transformations that have taken place over the years, Israeli strategic culture attitudes and approaches remained constant.

The Threat Perception and Warfighting Pattern of the Israeli Army

Given the strategic culture perception of Israeli politicians and military officers regarding national self-image, the siege mentality, on the one hand, and the image of aggressive and superior enemy generating a narrative of quantitative inferiority, on the other hand, caused the adoption of offensive pattern of conventional warfighting—Israel developed an offensive toolkit, with an escalation tendency and an emphasis on war preventing[141]:

---

[138] Maoz, *Defending the Holy Land*, 8.

[139] Tal, *National Security*, 69.

[140] The Israeli Defense Forces Strategy (2018, April), https://www.idf.il/media/34416/strategy.pdf. Accessed 26 December 2019.

[141] Haim Nadel (2006). *Between the Two Wars*, Tel Aviv: Maarachot, 48 [in Hebrew].

- Escalation through first strike concept
- Offensive strategy expressed by military decision effort
- Blitzkrieg—preference of short wars over protracted ones
- Transfer of war to the enemy's territory.

Due to the perception of geographical constraints of small territory and lack of strategic depth, a preemptive offensive was deemed as the optimal means for Israel's survival. The country cannot absorb fighting in its territory, not to mention the loss of territory. Accordingly, escalation and striking first is preferred and could increase the chances of demoralization of the enemy and achieving success at the battlefield.[142] One of the prominent architects of the first strike concept was Yigal Alon, who stated:

> ... Israel must have the moral right and operational capability to carry out a preemptive attack against an imminent attack. The necessity to advance the enemy is becoming increasingly vital as the danger increases that the enemy will use advanced weapons against Israeli vulnerable targets.[143]

One of the core stones of the Israeli military strategy is an offensive action:

> In order to impose our will on the enemy, the use of offensive force is required to achieve clear results.[144]

The central element of Israeli warfighting pattern is the decision. Decision on the strategic level is the negation of the enemy's fighting ability at the battlefield, by military means, that the recovery therefrom during a war has a very low probability.[145] In light of the abovementioned quantitative asymmetry, Israel couldn't achieve a final decision that would end the conflict with Arab states. According to the best-case scenario, the Israeli military could get a restricted decision, which doesn't deprive the possibility of the next round of war.[146]

---

[142] Avi Kober (2015). *Practical Soldiers*, Boston: Brill, 96.

[143] Alon, *Masah shel Hol*, 422.

[144] The Israeli Defense Forces Strategy.

[145] Kober, Military Decision in Israeli-Arabs Wars 1948–1982, 24.

[146] Kober, *Military Decision in Israeli-Arabs Wars 1948*–1982, 156.

Pursuant to the traditional view, one should strive not only to achieve military decision but to do so within a short period of time.[147] The need to quickly reach a decision is stemmed from Israel's inherent inability because of the power asymmetry to wage long wars.[148] Countries with limited resources and quantitative inferiority find it difficult to wage long wars. Additionally, protracted wars create a severe burden on the country's economy. The desire to reach a fast decision is also derived from the apprehension that an expected intervention by the superpowers was the "stopwatch" that could curtail Israel's achievements on the battlefield.[149] General Moshe Dayan, Chief of Staff of Israeli army and later Defense Minister, explained the matter as follows:

As of its earliest days, the Israeli army knew that it had to plan its battles and achieve its victories in a matter of days, because its government could not, for days, ignore the decisions of the international institutions and would not be able to resist the pressure of the great powers to stop the war.[150]

The practical expression of the decision concept was traditionally understood in terms of the destruction of force on the one hand, and the conquest of territories that Israel had not held before the war. Given Israel's small and narrow territory, the transfer of the war to enemy territory became an important principle in Israel's military doctrine.[151] Thus, from the very beginning of the state's existence, the idea of transferring the war to the enemy's territory was raised by Ben-Gurion:

If we are attacked and the war is once again imposed on us, we will not adopt a defensive strategy, but will proceed to attack the enemy - as far as possible in his territory ...[152]

---

[147] The Israeli Defense Forces Strategy.

[148] Kober, *Military Decision in Israeli-Arabs Wars 1948*–1982, 159.

[149] Yoav Ben–Horin & Barry Posen (1981). Israeli's Strategic Doctrine. Santa Monica: RAND, 7.

[150] Moshe Dayan (December 1986–January 1987). Sinai—After Ten Years, *Maarahot*, 306–307, 26–27.

[151] Nadel, *Between Two Wars*, 49.

[152] Nadel, *Between Two Wars*, 96.

As aforementioned, this approach is also reflected nowadays in the Israeli army strategy, which prescribes to transfer the combat to the other side's territory and to conduct the fighting there.[153]

Unlike Pakistan, despite similar weaknesses in terms of relative power *vis-à-vis* its enemies, Israel is an example of "*Nuclear Ignorance*" model, i.e., noninfluence of nuclear weaponization on its traditional pattern of warfighting. Such ignorance is due to the unchangeable relative power perception of Israeli political and military establishment. The nuclear weapon wasn't perceived as a deterrence factor and integrated in Israeli military doctrine, which remained merely based on conventional means. In Israel, the country that maintains the policy of nuclear ambiguity,[154] a nuclear weapon is not perceived by decision-makers as compensating for its abovementioned weakness. The way that the Israelis fought the conventional war in the post-weaponization period wasn't affected by the nuclear weaponization. Pursuant to the statements made by two senior IDF officers served during the Yom Kippur War of 1973—General Eli Zeira, head of the Intelligence Directorate, and Herzl Shafir, the head of the Manpower Directorate—weaponization could not have had any impact on the Israeli combat decisions, since it was never a factor in the decision-making process at the senior military command level.[155] In other words, the Israeli army "ignored" acquisition of such a destructive weapon.

[153] The Israeli Defense Forces Strategy.

[154] According to Israel's long-standing nuclear ambiguity policy formed in the 1960s, the country doesn't admit the existence of nuclear arsenal and will not be the first to introduce nuclear weapons into the Middle East region. See: Shimon Peres (1995). *Battling for Peace*, New York: Random House, 223.

[155] Ebridge Colby, Avner Cohen, William McCants, Bradley Morris, & William Rosenau (April 2013). *The Israeli "Nuclear Alert" of 1973: Deterrence and Signaling in Crisis*, CNA Analysis & Solutions, 44.

REFERENCES

Abbas, H. (2005). *Pakistan's Drift into Extremism*. New York: An East Gate Book.

Adamsky, D. (2012). *Strategic Culture and Military Innovation*. Ben Shemen: Modan Publishing [in Hebrew].

Aguilar, F., Bell, R., Black, N., et al. (2011). *An Introduction to Pakistan's Military*. Cambridge: Belfer Center for Science and International Affairs.

Ali, H. (June 2016). Economic Change in India Since Independence (1947–1965). *IRJIMS*, 2/4, 47–52.

Ansari, S. (1945). *Pakistan: The Problem of India*. Lahore: Minerva Book Shop.

Bajpai, K. (2002). Indian Strategic Culture. In Michael Chambers (Ed.), *South Asia in 2020: Future Strategic Balances and Alliances* (pp. 245–304). Carlisle, PA: Strategic Studies Institute.

Basrur, R. (March 2001). Nuclear Weapons and Indian Strategic Culture. *Journal of Peace Research*, 38/2, 181–198.

Baxter, C. (2015). Muhammad Ayub Khan. In Roger Long (Ed.), *A History of Pakistan* (pp. 485–512). Karachi: Oxford University Press.

Ben-Gurion, D. (1971). *Yiud i-Yihud*. Tel Aviv: Maarahot.

Ben-Gurion, D. (1981). Military and State. *Maarahot*, 280–279, 2–11 [in Hebrew].

Ben–Horin, Y. & Posen, B. (1981). *Israeli's Strategic Doctrine*. Santa Monica: RAND.

Bhargava, G. S. (1976). *India's Security in the 1980s*. London: The International Center for Strategic Studies.

Bhutto, Z. A. (1969). *The Myth of Independence*. London: Oxford University Press.

Cheema, P. I. (2002). *The Armed Forces of Pakistan*. New York: New York University Press.

Cohen, S. (1984). *The Pakistan Army*. Berkeley and Los Angeles: University of California Press.

Cohen, S. (2004). *The Idea of Pakistan*. Washington, DC: The Brookings Institution.

Cohen, S. & Dasgupta, S. (2013). *Arming Without Aiming*. Washington, DC: Brookings Institution Press.

Colby, E., Cohen, A., McCants, W., Morris, B. & Rosenau, W. (April 2013). *The Israeli "Nuclear Alert" of 1973: Deterrence and Signaling in Crisis*. CNA Analysis & Solutions.

Conley, J. (2001). *Indo-Russian Military and Nuclear Cooperation*. Lanham, MD: Lexington Books.

Das, P. (2010). Introduction. In Pushita Das (Ed.), *India's Border Management: Selected Documents* (pp. 1–40). New Delhi: Institute for Defense Studies and Analysis.

Fair, C. (2014). *Fighting to the End: The Pakistanis Army Way of War*. New York: Oxford University Press.

Ganguli, S. (1986). *The Origins of War in South Asia: Indo-Pakistani Conflicts Since 1947*. Boulder and London: Westview Press.

Ganguli, S. & Hagerty, D. (2005). *Fearful Symmetry: India-Pakistan Crises in the Shadow of Nuclear Weapons*. Seattle: University of Washington Press.

Ganguly, S. & Kapur, P. (2010). *India, Pakistan, and the Bomb*. New York: Columbia University Press.

Gauhar, A. (1996). *Ayub Khan: Pakistan's First Military Ruler*. Karachi: Oxford University Press.

Ghandi, I. (1972). *India and Bangla Desh: Selected Speeches and Statements, March to December 1971*. New Delhi: Orient Longman Limited.

Ghani, U. (September 2012). Nuclear Weapons in India-Pakistan Crisis. *IPRI Journal*, 2, 137–145.

Lt Gen. (Ret.) Habib, A. H. (1992). An Indonesian View of India's Strategic Development. In Ross Babbage & Sandy Gordon (Eds.), *India's Strategic Future* (pp. 107–121). Oxford: Oxford University Press.

Hanauer, L. & Chalk, P. (2012). *India's and Pakistan's Strategies in Afghanistan*. Santa Monica: RAND Center for Asia Pacific Policy.

Handel, M. (1994). The Evolution of Israeli Strategy: The Psychology of Insecurity and the Quest for Absolute Security. In Williamson Murray, Macgregor Knox, & Alvin Bernstein (Eds.), *The Making of Strategy* (pp. 534–578). New York: Cambridge University Press.

Hassan, P. (January 2007). State and Pakistan Economy: Where Have We Come From? Where Do We Go? www.economyofpakistan.blogspot.com/2007/01/state-and-pakistan-economy-where-have_22.html. Accessed 25 November 2019.

Horowitz, D. (1985). The Permanent and Changing Concept of Israeli Security. In Aharon Yariv & Yosef Alper (Eds.), *War of Choice* (pp. 11–57). Tel Aviv: Hakibbutz Hameuhad.

Jones, S. & Fair, C. (2010). *Counterinsurgency in Pakistan*. Santa Monica: RAND.

Joshua, A. (2011, 19 October). Pakistan Is Not Like Iraq or Afghanistan, Kayani Tells Washington. *The Hindu*, http://www.thehindu.com/news/international/pakistan-is-not-like-iraq-or-afghanistan-kayani-tells-washington/article2551586.ece. Accessed 4 August 2019.

Kapur, P. (Fall 2008). Ten Years of Instability in a Nuclear South Asia. *International Security*, 33/2, 71–94.

Kasturi, B. (2008). The State of War with Pakistan. In Daniel Martson & Chandar Sundaram (Eds.), *A Military History of India And South Asia* (pp. 139–156). Bloomington and Indianapolis: Indiana University Press.

Kavic, L. (1967). *India's Quest for Security: Defense Policies, 1947–1965.* Berkeley and Los Angeles: University of California Press.

Khan, F. H. (November 2005). Comparative Strategic Culture: The Case of Pakistan. *Strategic Insights,* 6/10, 1–13.

Khan, F. H. (2012). *Eating Grass: The Making of the Pakistani Bomb.* Stanford: Stanford University Press.

Khan, F. H. (September 2015). Going Tactical: Pakistan's Nuclear Posture and Implications for Stability. *Proliferation Paper,* 53, 1–44.

Lt. Col. Khan, K. M. (2015, October 16). The Strategic Depth Concept. *The Nation,* https://nation.com.pk/16-Oct-2015/the-strategic-depth-concept. Accessed 6 July 2019.

Khan, M. A. (2008). *Friends Not Masters.* Dhaka: The University Press Limited.

Kober, A. (1995). *Military Decision in Israeli-Arabs Wars 1948–1982.* Tel-Aviv: Maarachot [in Hebrew].

Lavoy, P. (31 October 2016). *Pakistan's Strategic Culture.* U.S. Defense Threat Reduction Agency.

Levita, A. (1988). *The Military Doctrine of Israel: Defense and Attack.* Tel Aviv: Hakibbutz Hameuhad [in Hebrew].

Ludwig, W. (Winter 2007/2008). A Cold Start for Hot Wars? *International Security,* 32/3, 158–190.

General Malik, V. P. (2006). *Kargil: From Surprise to Victory.* New Delhi: HarperCollins Publishers India.

General Malik, V. P. (2016). *India's Military Conflicts and Diplomacy.* New Delhi: HarperCollins Publishers India.

Mandelbaum, M. (1989). *The Fate of Nations: The Search for National Security in the Nineteenth and Twentieth Centuries.* Cambridge: Cambridge University Press.

Maoz, Z. (2009). *Defending the Holy Land.* Ann Arbor: The University of Michigan Press.

Mason, S. (2016). *Military Budgets in India and Pakistan: Trajectories, Priorities and Risks.* Washington, DC: Stimson Center.

Musharraf, P. (2006). *In the Line of Fire.* London: Simon & Shuster UK Ltd.

Nadel, H. (2006). *Between the Two Wars.* Tel Aviv: Maarachot [in Hebrew].

Narang, V. (2014). *Nuclear Strategy in the Modern Era.* Princeton and Oxford: Princeton University Press.

Nawaz, S. (2008). *Crossed Swords: Pakistan, Its Army, and the Wars Within.* Oxford: Oxford University Press.

Ogden, C. (2014). *Indian Foreign Policy: Ambition and Transition.* Cambridge: Polity Press.

Panhwar, S. H. (2009). *Benazir Bhutto: Selected Speeches 1989–2007,* http://bhutto.org/Acrobat/BB_Speeches_Book.pdf. Accessed 3 August 2019.

Parkes, A. (2019). Considered Chaos: Revisiting Pakistan's "Strategic Depth" in Afghanistan. *Strategic Studies*, 1–13.

Peres, S. (1995). *Battling for Peace*. New York: Random House.

Qureshi, I. H. (1956). *The Pakistani Way of Life*. New York: Frederick A. Praeger.

Radcliffe, R. & Baloch, S. M. (2019, August 11). Imran Khan Likens Inaction Over Kashmir to Appeasing Hitler. *The Guardian*, https://www.theguardian.com/world/2019/aug/11/imran-khan-likens-global-inaction-on-kashmir-to-appeasing-hitler. Accessed 12 August 2019.

Commodore Richards, K. (February 2015). *China-India: An Analysis of the Himalayan Territorial Dispute*. Australian Defense College, Center for Defense and Strategic Studies.

Rizvi, H. A. (2002). Pakistan's Strategic Culture. In Michael Chambers (Ed.), *South Asia in 2020: Future Strategic Balances and Alliances* (pp. 305–328). Carlisle, PA: Strategic Studies Institute.

Rodman, D. (September 2001). Israel's National Security Doctrine: An Introductory Overview. *Middle East Review of International Affairs*, 5/3, 71–86.

Rotem, A. (2002). A Smart Small Army—Vision or Legend? In Haggai Golan (Ed.), *Israel's Security Web: Core Issues of Israel's National Security in Its Sixth Decade* (pp. 71–93). Tel Aviv: Maarahot [in Hebrew].

Shahid, K. K. (2017, March 16). Nawaz Sharif's Historic Holi Address. *The Diplomat*, https://thediplomat.com/2017/03/nawaz-sharifs-historic-holi-address. Accessed 28 July 2019.

Shahzad, A. (2019, August 6). Pakistan Army Chief Says Military Will "Go to Any Extent" to Support Kashmir Cause. *Reuters*, https://www.reuters.com/article/us-india-kashmir-pakistan-army/pakistan-army-chief-says-military-will-go-to-any-extent-to-support-kashmir-cause-idUSKCN1UW0ZM. Accessed 12 August 2019.

Shukla, A. (July–September 2011). Pakistan's Quest for Strategic Depth: Regional Security Implications. *Himalayan and Central Asian Studies*, 15/3, 81–104.

Siddiqa-Agha, A. (2001). *Pakistan's Arms Procurement and Military Buildup, 1979–99*. New York: Palgrave.

Simchoni, A. (2006). *Strategic Depth and the Eastern Front*. Tel Aviv: Tel Aviv University [in Hebrew].

Singh, H. (2009). *India's Strategic Culture: The Impact of Geography*. New Delhi: Center for Land Warfare Studies.

Sing, J. (1999). *Defending India*. Bangalore: Macmillan India Ltd.

Sondhause, L. (2006). *Strategic Culture and Ways of War*. Abingdon, Oxon: Routledge.

Sukumaram, R. (July–September 2003). The 1962 India-China War and Kargil 1999: Restrictions of the Use of Air Power. *Strategic Analysis*, 27/3, 332–356.

Tal, I. (1996). *National Security: Few vs. Many*. Tel Aviv: Dvir [in Hebrew].

Tanham, G. (1992). *Indian Strategic Thought*. Santa Monica: RAND.

Tira, R. (September 2008). *The Struggle for the Nature of War*. Tel Aviv: National Security Research Institute.

Verzberger, Y. (1984). *Misperceptions in Foreign Policymaking: The Sino-Indian Conflict, 1959–1962*. Boulder: Westview Press.

Weinbaum, M. & Harder, J. (March 2008). Pakistan's Afghan Policies and Their Consequences. *Contemporary South Asia*, 16/1, 25–38.

Yaniv, A. (1994). *Politics and Strategy in Israel*. Tel Aviv: Sifriyat Poalim [in Hebrew].

Zeira, E. (2004). *Myth vs. Reality*. Tel Aviv: Miskal [in Hebrew].

The Israeli Defense Forces Strategy. (2018, April). https://www.idf.il/media/34416/strategy.pdf. Accessed 26 December 2019.

India Is the Only External Threat, Says Military. (2015, 28 August). *DAWN*. https://www.dawn.com/news/1203329. Accessed 4 August 2019.

India Population. World Bank. https://data.worldbank.org/indicator/SP.POP.TOTL?locations=IN&view=chart. Accessed 18 November 2019.

Jawaharlal Nehru's Speeches, August 1949–February 1953. (1954). New Delhi: Publications Division.

Kashmir Is a Core Dispute Between Pakistan and India. (2017, February 2). *Times of India*, http://timesofindia.indiatimes.com/world/pakistan/kashmir-is-core-dispute-between-india-and-pakistan-nawaz-sharif/articleshow/56982014.cms. Accessed 12 August 2019.

Message from Prime Minister Imran Khan on Birth Anniversary of Quaid-e-Azam. (2019, December 25). https://www.facebook.com/ImranKhanOfficial/posts/message-ofprime-minister-of-the-islamic-republic-of-pakistanmr-imran-khanon-the-/3144165112292554. Accessed 25 December 2019.

Narendra Modi Speech. (2019, August 8). https://www.narendramodi.in/prime-minister-narendra-modi-s-address-to-the-nation-on-8th-august-2019-545901. Accessed 26 August 2019.

Pakistan Should Protect Its National Interest Over Middle East Crisis. (2020, January 7). *DAWN*, https://www.dawn.com/news/1526716/pakistan-should-protect-its-national-interest-over-middle-east-crisis. Accessed 8 January 2020.

General Raheel Sharif: Pakistan Will Continue to Support Kashmir on Diplomatic Front. (2016, September 7). *Indian Express*, http://indianexpres.com/article/world-news/pakistan-kashmir-dispute. Accessed 12 August 2019.

Premier-Minister Netanyahu's Speech on Holocaust Remembrance Day at Yad Vashem. (2017, April 23). http://www.pmo.gov.il/MediaCenter/Speeches/Pages/speechYadVashem230417.aspx. Accessed 5 September 2019 [in Hebrew].

Presidential Address by Muhammad Ali Jinnah to the Muslim League, Lahore, 1940. http://columbia.edu/itc/mealac/pritchett/00islaminks/txt_jinnah_lohore_1940.html. Accessed 27 July 2019.

Selected Speeches and Writings of Indira Gandhi, September 1972–March 1977. (1984). New Delhi: Publications Division.

Selected Works of Jawaharlal Nehru, 26 October 1950–28 February 1951. (1993). New Delhi: Jawaharlal Nehru Memorial Fund.

U.S. Foreign Aid to Israel. (2019, August 7). Congressional Research Service, https://fas.org/sgp/crs/mideast/RL33222.pdf. Accessed 27 November 2019.

CHAPTER 5

Nuclear Development Programs: Historical Insight

Abstract In this chapter we will briefly review the history of the nuclear development of the three countries in order to identify the time period in which each of the case studies crossed the nuclear weaponization threshold. This identification is necessary in order to determine chronologically which conventional wars, fought by the three countries, occurred either in the pre- or post-weaponization periods. A common characteristic of the examined countries is that they have launched the development of their nuclear capability upon the occurrence of various tragic and dramatic events in their history. While in the Israeli and Pakistani cases it was the traumatic events of Holocaust and the Indian conventional superiority, respectively, which caused decision-makers in these countries to initiate a nuclear program and subsequently to cross the weaponization threshold. In the Indian case study it was the defeat in a war with communist China, which forced decision-makers in New Delhi to reexamine their antinuclear rhetoric.

Keywords "Atoms for Peace" · Nuclear ambiguity · "Smiling Buddha" · Vela incident

In this chapter I will briefly review the history of the nuclear development of the three countries in order to identify the time period in which each of the case studies crossed the nuclear weaponization threshold.

This identification is necessary in order to determine chronologically which conventional wars, fought by the three countries, occurred either in the pre- or post-weaponization periods.

A common characteristic of the examined countries is that they have launched the development of their nuclear capability upon the occurrence of various tragic and dramatic events in their history. Feroz Hassan Khan defined this dynamic as a "Never Again Narrative." According to this approach:

> At the core of the nuclear weapons acquisition narrative rests national humiliation- the phrase 'never again" is repeated over and over in nuclear histories.[1]

While in the Israeli and Pakistani cases it was traumatic events of Holocaust and the Indian conventional superiority, respectively, which caused decision-makers in these countries to initiate a nuclear program and subsequently cross the weaponization threshold, in the Indian case study it was the defeat in a war with communist China, which forced decision-makers in New Delhi to reexamine their antinuclear rhetoric.

PAKISTAN

The main motive behind Pakistani desire to obtain nuclear weapons was the sense of threat from India and the conventional asymmetry at the conventional level, which was clearly in favor of the Indian army. Since the independence, Islamabad's defense policy was determined by the Indian threat. A decision to develop a nuclear weapon and subsequently to cross the nuclear weaponization threshold reflect the same.[2] In 1966, in light of reports of India's nuclear development program, Pakistani Foreign Minister Zulfikar Ali Bhutto declared that if India continued to develop a nuclear option, Pakistan would do so: "even if Pakistanis have to eat grass, we will make the bomb."[3] Many years later, in 2011, Pakistani scientist Abdul Qadir Khan, known as the "father of

[1] Khan, *Eating Grass*, 7.

[2] Iram Khalid & Zakia Bano (January–June 2015). Pakistan's Nuclear Development (1974–1998): External Pressures, *South Asian Studies*, 30/1, 221.

[3] Thomas Reed & Danny Stillman (2009). *The Nuclear Express*, Minnesota: Zenith Press, 183.

the Pakistani bomb," in an interview to the German newspaper "Der Spiegel," reiterated the same position, suggesting that Pakistan's nuclear program was a response to the nuclear test conducted by its neighbor, India.[4]

Already in the early 1950s, the Pakistani military establishment began to address the issue of the modern battlefield, in which nuclear weapons played a central role. The commander of the Pakistan Army Command and Staff College, General Latif Khan, recalled that when he took office in 1954, he appointed a senior officer to deal with the issue:

> On taking over as Commandant I found that the study of the various operations of war under nuclear conditions was carried out in an elementary form and a few enquiries made by me soon revealed the fact that this subject had not received the attention it deserved. The time had come for us to start making a serious study of fighting the next war which would, whether we liked it or not, be fought with nuclear weapons.[5]

Similarly to India and Israel, Pakistan began its nuclear development as a civilian program, within the framework of the US "Atoms for Peace" initiative of President Dwight Eisenhower administration. The American goal was to create incentives for states to refrain from developing nuclear weapons by providing assistance in building nuclear energy facilities for civilian purposes and sharing knowledge in the field. One of the fist main official statements on Pakistan's nuclear program was made on January 1, 1955 by Prime Minister Mohammad Ali:

> A step forward in the scientific field was the formulation of a scheme to set up a Nuclear Research Center for exploring the possibility of obtaining uranium from the mountainous regions of our country with a view to production of atomic energy for the country's economic development.[6]

[4]Vielleict Sind Wiir Naiv, Idioten Sind Wir Nicht (2011, June 27). *Der Spiegel*, http://m.spiegel.de/politik/ausland/pakistans-atombombe-vielleicht-sind-wir-naiv-idioten-sind-wir-nicht-a-770498.html. Accessed 5 September 2019 [in German].

[5]Zia Mian (2009). Fevered with Dreams of the Future: The Coming of the Atomic Age to Pakistan, in Itty Abraham (Ed.), *South Asian Cultures of the Bomb*, Bloomington: Indiana University Press, 26.

[6]Mian, Fevered with Dreams of the Future, 34.

The Pakistan Atomic Energy Commission (PAEC) was established in 1957 and has served as a platform for training scientists and promoting research.[7] Similarly to other developing countries at the time, Pakistan sent in 1955–1974, scientists for training in the United States, France, Canada, Britain, the Soviet Union, and the International Atomic Energy Agency (IAEA).[8] On August 11, 1955, Pakistan and the United States signed an agreement which established nuclear cooperation between the countries for civilian purposes.[9] Under the aforementioned agreement, the United States has undertaken to provide research facilities and assist in the design, construction, and operation of power stations, in a total amount of up to $350,000. It should be noted that PAEC wanted to receive a more powerful reactor. It did not happen, however, due to financial constraints and the refusal of Americans, which feared that an upgraded infrastructure would be used for military purposes.[10] Additionally, in the 1960s Islamabad also signed cooperation agreements with Canada for the purposes of construction of the civil nuclear infrastructure.[11]

At first, in the 1950s and 1960s, Pakistan's nuclear weapons policy was characterized by a policy of maintaining an "open option," which meant that if needed, Islamabad would reconsider its nuclear policy. This policy was reflected in Pakistan's refusal to sign the NPT in 1968, mainly due to New Delhi's refusal to accede to this international agreement.[12] Furthermore, during the aforementioned period Pakistan began to worry that its neighbor India was engaged in nuclear weapons development. This concern was reinforced in 1965 in light of the notification that India had commenced construction of the plutonium separation facility.[13] Years later, former Foreign Minister Agha Shahi said that

[7] Samina Ahmed (Spring 1999). Pakistan's Nuclear Weapons Program, *International Security*, 23/4, 181.

[8] Bhumitra Chakma (2010). *Pakistan's Nuclear Weapons*, London and New York: Routledge, 12.

[9] Shahid ur-Rehman (1999). *Long Road to Chagai*, Islamabad: Print Wise Publication, 22.

[10] Khan, *Eating Grass*, 29–30.

[11] Frantz Douglas & Catherine Collins (2007). *The Nuclear Jihadist*, New York: Twelve, 20.

[12] Bhumitra Chakma (2011). The Pakistani Nuclear Deterrent, in Bhumitra Chakma (Ed.), *The Politics of Nuclear Weapons in South Asia*, Cornwall: TJ International, 40.

[13] Chakma, The Pakistani Nuclear Deterrent, 41.

during the visit of Pakistani leader Field marshal Ayoub Khan in Paris in the 1960s, several officials in the Pakistani Foreign Ministry suggested to ask the French to supply a plutonium production facility, but the issue wasn't eventually raised by Khan.[14]

Finally, the decision to develop nuclear weapons was made during a secret meeting of senior scientists held in Multan in 1972, a year after the defeat in the war against India.[15] During such a meeting, the Pakistani leader Bhutto required that the participants would produce a bomb within three years and declared that for the purpose of the mission, the state would not save any resources and infrastructure.[16]

The main purpose behind the effort to achieve nuclear capability was to balance the quantitative advantage of Indian conventional forces.[17] The factor that served as an additional incentive for the development of nuclear weapons in Pakistan was the Indian nuclear test, held on May 18, 1974. The test which was called the "Smiling Buddha," was conducted on the Pokhran site, located about 100 km from the international border with Pakistan, in the Rajasthan desert. The Indians defined the test as a peaceful one. This, however, did not relieve the concerns of the Pakistanis. The day after the test, Bhutto convened a press conference during which he declared that his country would not tolerate Indian hegemony in the subcontinent:

> Let me make it clear that we are determined not to be intimidated by this threat. I give a solemn pledge to all our countrymen that we will never let Pakistan be a victim of nuclear blackmail. This means not only that we will never surrender our rights or claims because of India's nuclear status, but also that we will not be deflected from our policies by this fateful development. In concrete terms, we will not compromise the right of self-determination of the people of Jammu and Kashmir. Nor will we accept Indian hegemony over the Sub-continent.[18]

[14] ur-Rehman, *Long Road to Chagai*, 20.

[15] Paul Kerr & Mary Beth Nikitin (August 2016). *Pakistan's Nuclear Weapons*, Congressional Research Service, 2.

[16] Gordon Corera (2006). *Shopping for Bombs*, Oxford: Oxford University Press, 10.

[17] K. Subrahmanyan (2002). India and the International Nuclear Order, in Damodar Sardesai & Raju Thomas (Eds.), *Nuclear India in the Twenty First Century*, New York: Palgrave Macmillan, 75.

[18] Khan, *Eating Grass*, 118.

Bhutto also noted that India's declarations that the test was for peace purposes only were not reassured and that the military and civilian features of a nuclear program should not be separated.[19]

The Pakistani official position remained that the country's nuclear program was for peaceful purposes only.[20] It was an expression of a nuclear ambiguity policy adopted by Pakistan, which was concerned about the international pressure. Is should be noted that when the decision to develop the nuclear program in 1971 was made, the NPT was already in force, thereby making it difficult to openly develop a military nuclear program.

In order to finance the ambitious program, Pakistan labeled the nuclear project as an "Islamic bomb," which would award the Muslim world the respect it deserves. Subsequently, Bhutto appealed to the various Muslim countries in the world to raise funds for a potential nuclear project. As Feroz Hassan Khan outlined:

> Bhutto cleverly embroidered the Pakistani nuclear program with an Islamic identity and attracted support from Saudi Arabia and Libya, in particular. Bhutto boasted that he would make Pakistan the first Muslim nuclear power, rhetoric that resonated both.[21]

To circumvent international restrictions and to obtain sensitive technologies, Pakistan approached its ally, China.[22] According to the secret documents released for publication, as early as the 1970s the US intelligence agency received information about Chinese aid to the Pakistani nuclear program, which included the transfer of sensitive information related to nuclear weapon development.[23] In May 2004, in a letter to his wife, Dr. Abdul Qadir Khan addressed the relationship with China in the

[19] Nuclear Chronology 1970–1974, http://www.bhutto.org/article21.php. Accessed 11 September 2019.

[20] Khalid & Bano (January–June 2015). Pakistan's Nuclear Development, 227.

[21] Khan, *Eating Grass*, 12.

[22] Feroz Hassan Khan (2009). Pakistan's Perspective on the Global Elimination of Nuclear Weapons, in Barry Blechman (Ed.), *Pakistan and Israel*, Washington: The Henry L. Stimson Center, 13.

[23] William Burr (2016, May 18). National Security Archive, *Electronic Book*, 59, http://nsarchive.gwu.edu/nukevault/ebb549-INRs-NuclearWatch-1957-1967. Accessed 11 September 2011.

nuclear field, noting that the Chinese have handed over to Pakistan nuclear weapons drawings, 50 kilograms of enriched uranium, and more.[24]

An important milestone in the Pakistani nuclear project was the success of an independent enrichment of uranium. In January 1984, in an interview given to Quami Digest, published in Urdu, Pakistan's official language, Dr. Khan openly stated that Pakistan had acquired the ability to enrich uranium.[25] This has become a symbol of national pride and technological progress and practically has ended Pakistan's dependence on foreign sources.

On May 28 and 30, 1998, Pakistan conducted public nuclear tests in Chagai, in Baluchistan province. It was a reaction to a previous Indian nuclear experiment. According to a senior Pakistani politician, Satraj Aziz:

> Pakistan was only [the] dependent variable responding to India's "independent" decision to exercise its "nuclear option".[26]

Nevertheless, such public nuclear tests did not mean the acquisition of a military nuclear capability, which has had in fact confidentially occurred earlier. Pakistan has become a nuclear-armed state, namely crossed the nuclear weaponization threshold before conducting public tests. Nevertheless, due to the nuclear ambiguity policy that was in effect until the nuclear tests of 1998, it is not possible to determine precisely when Pakistan crossed the nuclear weaponization threshold and the assessments in this regard may vary. While some scholars have argued that Pakistan carried out the weaponization in the late 1980s,[27] whereas others assumed that it happened in 1987.[28] It should be noted that at the

---

[24] Khan, *Eating Grass*, 188.

[25] Khan, *Eating Grass*, 160.

[26] Khan, Going Tactical, 7.

[27] See for example: Farah Zarah (2000). Pakistan's Elusive Search for Nuclear Parity with India, in Raju Thomas & Amit Gupta (Eds.), *India's Nuclear Security*, Boulder, CO: Lynne Rienner, 147; Pervaiz Iqbal Cheema (2011). Nuclear and Missile Developments, in Scott Gates & Kaushik Roy (Eds.), *The Nuclear Shadow Over South Asia, 1947 to the Present*, Farnham: Ashgate, 243; Paul Kapur (2009). Revisionist Ambitions, Conventional Capabilities, and Nuclear Instability. Why Nuclear Asia Is Not Like Cold War Europe, in Scott Sagan (Ed.), *Inside Nuclear South Asia*, Stanford, CA: Stanford University Press, 185.

[28] See for example: Saira Khan (2009). *Nuclear Weapons and Conflict Transformation. The Case of India-Pakistan*, London: Routledge, 68; Chakma, The Pakistani Nuclear Deterrence, 44–45; K. Subrahmanyam, India and the International Nuclear Order, 75.

same time, Abdul Qadir Khan in an interview to the Pakistani newspaper "Muslim" confirmed that Pakistan has a nuclear bomb:

> Nobody can undo Pakistan or take us for granted. We are here to stay and let it be clear that we shall use the bomb if our existence is threatened. They told us that Pakistan could never produce the bomb and they doubted my capabilities, but now they know we have done it... America knows it. What CIA has been saying about our possessing the bomb is correct and so is speculation in some foreign newspapers.[29]

Despite the lack of clarity regarding the exact timing of crossing the nuclear weaponization threshold by Islamabad and in light of Dr. Khan's declaration supported by several researchers, I assume that Pakistan achieved weaponization in 1987.

INDIA

The Indian nuclear program began even before the declaration of independence in 1947 under the leadership of the renowned physicist Homi Bhabha. In 1944, he initiated the establishment of a nuclear research center.[30] Bhabha persuaded the Tata family, the local industrialists, to donate funds to set up a nuclear physics research center. The Tata Research Center was opened in Bombay in 1945 and after the declaration of the Independence received the support of Prime Minister Jawaharlal Nehru.[31] Upon the establishment of the state, the prominent scientist was appointed as the head of the Atomic Energy Commission of India, which was established on August 10, 1948, the first anniversary of India's independence.[32]

Initially, India's attitude to nuclear weapons was affected by the views of Mahatma Gandhi, which stated in 1947 that nuclear weapons

[29] Leonard Spector (1988). *The Undeclared Bomb*, Cambridge, MA: Ballinger Publishing Company, 103.

[30] Stephen Cohen (2011). India as a Nuclear Power, in Scott Gates & Kaushik Roy (Eds.), *The Nuclear Shadow Over South Asia, 1947 to the Present*, Farnham: Ashgate, 157.

[31] Samit Ganguly (2000). Explaining the Indian Nuclear Tests of 1998, in Raju Thomas & Amit Gupta (Eds.), *India's Nuclear Security*, Boulder, CO: Lynne Rienner, 39.

[32] Itty Abraham (1998). *The Making of the Indian Atomic Bomb*, London and New York: ZED Books, 61.

constituted a false and diabolical exploitation of science.[33] At first, as an independent state, India has promoted the idea of nuclear disarmament in the world. Pursuant to such policy in respect of nuclear development, India became the first country in the world to call in 1954 a ban on nuclear tests in the world.[34] In the first edition of the study initiated by Nehru regarding the implications of nuclear explosion, he stated:

> We now have to face death on a colossal scale and, what is much worse, the genetic efforts of these explosions on the present and future generations. Before this prospect, the other problems that face us in this world relatively unimportant. But even without war we have what are called nuclear test explosions which, in some measure, spread this level thing over large parts of the world.[35]

Notwithstanding the foregoing, regardless of the clear antinuclear line adopted by the Indian officials, India has launched a nuclear development program. Despite the declarations that nuclear energy will drive India toward progress, Bhabha led and strived to develop dual nuclear capabilities that could be potentially used for both military and peace purposes. Nehru also, despite his antimilitaristic rhetoric, did not rule out the possibility that India would develop military nuclear capability at some point of time.[36] In his speech held on August 10, 1960 at the Parliament, he stated:

> So far as we are concerned, we are determined not to go in for making atomic bombs and the like... And no declaration which I can make today will necessarily bind people in future, but I do hope that we shall create an atmosphere in this country which will bind every Government in future not to use this power for evil purposes.[37]

[33] Praful Bidwai & Achin Vanaik (2000). *New Nukes*, New York: Interlink Publishing Group, Inc., 129.

[34] Or Rabinowitz (2014). *Bargaining on Nuclear Tests: Washington and Its Cold War Deals*, Oxford: Oxford University Press, 171.

[35] Cohen, India as a Nuclear Power, 163.

[36] George Perkovich (2002). What Makes the Indian Bomb Tick, in Damodar Sardesai & Raju Thomas (Eds.), *Nuclear India in the Twenty First Century*, New York: Palgrave Macmillan, 27.

[37] *Jawaharlal Nehru's Speeches, September 1957–April 1963* (1964). New Delhi: Ministry of Information and Broadcasting, 436.

Despite the local research infrastructure, India similarly to Pakistan did not promote its nuclear ambitions based solely on its local capabilities, but also obtained foreign assistance from Britain, France and the United States. India, as well as its neighbor, has made progress in nuclear research and development, within the framework of the American "Atoms for Peace" cooperation program. Due to this scientific cooperation many Indian nuclear scientists completed training at American research facilities.[38] Additionally, New Delhi has established a nuclear cooperation with France and Canada.

India's desire to promote nuclear energy was not initially derived from any military threat but was more based on the interest to establish its status as a progressive country. It was the loss in a border war with communist China in 1962, which inflamed the debate over the need for a nuclear weapon.[39] This military defeat forced Indian decision-makers to seriously examine the possibility of utilization of nuclear capabilities for military purposes. In 1964, China conducted a nuclear test at Lop Nur site and thus joined the club of nuclear-armed countries. This event was perceived as a watershed in the South Asian region and increased the sense of threat in New Delhi.[40] The Prime Minister of India at the time, Lal Bahadur Shastri, defined the test as "astonishment and danger to world peace."[41] Nevertheless, although Beijing's nuclear test contributed to the New Delhi's decision to proceed with is nuclear endeavors, it didn't result in the decision to develop a nuclear project for military purposes.

In 1966, after the death of Shastri, Indira Gandhi, a daughter of Nehru, was elected to the Prime Minister post. During her term, the nuclear research and development continued. In September 1972, Indira Gandhi instructed the Atomic Energy Commission to prepare a nuclear device for a peaceful test.[42] The test, which has been called the "Smiling Buddha," was held on May 18, 1974, at Pokhran site. Immediately afterwards, the

---

[38] George Perkovich (1999). *India's Nuclear Bomb*, Los Angeles: University of California Press, 30.

[39] Arpit Rajain (2005). *Nuclear Deterrence in Southern Asia*, New Delhi: Sage, 208.

[40] T. V. Paul (2002). India, the International System and Nuclear Weapons, in Damodar Sardesai & Raju Thomas (Eds.), *Nuclear India in the Twenty First Century*, New York: Palgrave Macmillan, 92.

[41] Perkovich, *India's Nuclear Bomb*, 66.

[42] Perkovich, What Makes the Indian Bomb Tick, 33.

radio station "All India Radio" released a special announcement regarding the event:

> At 8:05 a.m. this morning, India successfully conducted an underground nuclear explosion for peaceful purposes at a carefully chosen site.[43]

It should be noted that the device that was detonated was rather a "gadget" than an operational weapon.[44] It was similar to the one that was detonated in the American Trinity test on July 16, 1945.[45] Although the test marked a significant progress in nuclear development endeavors, India has not progressed and crossed the nuclear weaponization threshold.[46] Gandhi's government interpreted the test as a political act to demonstrate the national prestige rather than as a response to the Chinese threat.[47] In the period after the "Smiling Buddha", India proceeded with the self-restraint policy, which slowly began to crack in view of the reports pertaining to the progress of the Pakistani nuclear program.

In the meantime, India's nuclear capabilities developed significantly during the 1980s. In an interview to the French magazine "Le Monde" in 1984 the Indian Prime Minister Rajiv Gandhi, Indira Gandhi's son, noted that should his country decide to become a nuclear power, it will take several weeks or even months.[48] Later in 1985, in a specific reference to the Pakistani nuclear threat, Gandhi has stated that in light of progress in nuclear capabilities development in Pakistan, India is reconsidering its traditional commitment not to develop a nuclear bomb.[49] Two years later, in 1987,India's then president, Zail Singh, reiterated in an interview with the newspaper "Times of India" that if required India

---

[43] Khan, *Eating Grass*, 117.

[44] Reed & Stillman, *The Nuclear Express*, 237.

[45] C. Ashtana & Anjali Nirmal (2012). *Indian Defense: Crisis and Challenges*, Jaipur: Pointer Publishers, 201.

[46] Carranza, *South Asian Security and International Nuclear Oder*, 1.

[47] Spector, *The Undeclared Bomb*, 82.

[48] Spector, *The Undeclared Bomb*, 85.

[49] Davin Hagerty (1998). *The Consequences of Nuclear Proliferation*, Cambridge: The MIT Press, 84.

could also produce a bomb and the surrounding countries trying to destabilize the region should take this into account.[50]

Although India's nuclear weapon program received a significant boost during Gandhi's term as Prime Minister, there are various assessments regarding the period in which the country crossed the nuclear weaponization threshold. As its neighbor Pakistan, New Delhi crossed the nuclear weaponization threshold before conducting public nuclear tests in 1998. Some scientists referred to 1986–1988 as a period when the nuclear weaponization occurred.[51] Others argued that Prime Minister Gandhi instructed to begin the weaponization process in 1988, pointing to 1990 as the year in which India conducted weaponization.[52]

There is no doubt that nuclear ambiguity policy adopted by the Indian government throughout the years, makes it difficult to specify exactly when India crossed the nuclear weaponization threshold. Notwithstanding the differences among the researchers it is clear that in the late 1980s, the Indian nuclear program reached a high level of development. Despite the lack of clarity, it can be concluded that around 1990 India became a nuclear-armed country. Therefore, I assume that India crossed the nuclear weaponization threshold in this period.

Israel

The main cause for Israeli decision-makers' motivation to obtain a nuclear weapon was a significant conventional threat of the Arab armies. Given Israel's inferiority in terms of relative power *vis-à-vis* Arab states, Ben-Gurion was concerned about the possibility that in the future the Arabs would unite and initiate a total war against the state.[53] Until the

---

[50] Perkovich, India's Nuclear Bomb, 284.

[51] See for example: Itty Abraham (2009). Contra-Proliferation, in Scott Sagan (Ed.), *Inside Nuclear South Asia*, Stanford, CA: Stanford University Press, 119; Rajesh Basrur (2008). *South Asia's Cold War*, London and New York: Routledge, 55; D.C. Ashtana & Nirmal, *Indian Defense*, 201.

[52] See for example: Rabinowitz, *Bargaining on Nuclear Tests*, 180; Raja Mohan (1998). India and Nuclear Weapons, *Internationale Politik und Geselschaft*, 4, 377; Verghese Koithara (2012). *Managing India's Nuclear Forces*, Washington, DC: Brookings Institution Press, 95; Nischal Nath Pandey & Bhumitra Chakma (2011). Nuclear Proliferation in South Asia and Its Impact on Regional Cooperation, in Bhumitra Chakma (Ed.), *The Politics of Nuclear Weapons in South Asia*, Farnham: Ashgate, 140.

[53] David Ben-Gurion (1975). *Behilahem Am Israel*, Tel Aviv: Am Oved, 39 [in Hebrew].

Sinai Campaign in 1956, Ben-Gurion considered the Egyptian President Nasser as having the potential to become a leader able to unite Arab countries against the Jewish state. In Ben-Gurion's view, however, these fears started to fade away after the 1956 Sinai Campaign.[54]

From his point of view, the nuclear option would provide the ability to deal with the threat of quantitative asymmetry of the Arab armies, thereby convincing the Arab states of the futility of efforts to militarily defeat Israel.[55] Adam Raz, in his book on the political disputes over the development of the Israeli nuclear weapon program, stated that for the Defense Minister, Shimon Peres and the Chief of Staff, General Moshe Dayan—both leading supports of the initiative to acquire nuclear weapons—the conventional arms race *vis-à-vis* the Arab states, especially Egypt, was hopeless because the Arabs would always benefit from a quantitative advantage *vis-à-vis* Israel.[56] Peres referred in 1962 to the need of obtaining nonconventional equipment as follows:

> Israel must ensure for itself the ability to manage any possible threat that may lead to an attack on it. That means it must equip itself with the advanced conventional and non-conventional weapons.[57]

Additionally, the desire of Israel's first Prime Minister David Ben-Gurion to achieve the nuclear capability stemmed from the deep fear regarding the future of the Jewish people.[58] The Israeli leader was affected by the events of the Holocaust. In the early 1950s, in light of a domestic political crisis pertaining to the Reparations Agreement with West Germany, the Prime Minister declared that Israel should receive financial aid from Germany to prevent a situation in which Jews would again be helpless:

[54] Zaki Shalom (2005). *Israel's Nuclear Option*, Portland and Tel Aviv: Sussex Academic Press and JCSS, 2.

[55] Shai Feldman (1997). *Nuclear Weapons and Arms Control in the Middle East*, Massachusetts: Harvard University, 95–96.

[56] Adam Raz (2015). *Hamaavak al Hapzaza*, Jerusalem: Carmel, 151 [in Hebrew].

[57] Raz, *Hamaavak al Hapzaza*, 107.

[58] Rabinowitz, *Bargaining on Nuclear Tests*, 72.

> They [Arabs] could slaughter us in this country. We don't want to reach
> again the situation that you were in. We don't want the Arab Nazis come
> and slaughter us.[59]

Already during the Independence war, the Israeli Prime Minister initiated an Israeli development program.[60] The catalyst for a nuclear research program was the discovery of limited deposits of uranium in phosphates in the Negev.[61] As early as 1949, at the Weizmann Institute of Science a nuclear research laboratory was founded.[62] On June 13, 1952, the Atomic Energy Commission was established, headed by Ernst David Bergman. Along with the Pakistani and Indian case studies, the Israeli nuclear program first began as a civil initiative, supported by the Eisenhower administration's "Atoms for Peace" program of the 1950s. Within such a program, the Americans proposed in 1954 to build a small research reactor, which would eventually be built in Nahal Soreq, southern to Tel Aviv. It is noteworthy that Israel was the second country to join the American initiative, after Turkey.[63] On July 12, 1955, the agreement was signed between Israel and the United States, in the framework of which cooperation in the field of nuclear energy for peaceful purposes was established.

Another cooperation was established with France. While cooperation with the United States revolves around nuclear research for peaceful purposes only, the cooperation with France was characterized by secrecy and was derived from entirely different purposes—the development of nuclear weapon arsenal. In September 1956, a few weeks before the beginning of the Sinai Campaign, a joint Israeli–French–British military operation against Egypt, Ben-Gurion decided to approach the French government to assist in the development of Israeli nuclear weapons.[64] The secret nuclear cooperation between Tel Aviv and Paris continued until the mid-1960s. Years later, the then head of the French Atomic Energy Commission,

---

[59] Avner Cohen (1998). *Israel and the Bomb*, New York: Columbia University Press, 13.

[60] Shlomo Aronson (2014). *Nuclear Weapon in the Middle East, 1948–2013*, Jerusalem: Magnes, 29.

[61] Evron, *Israel's Nuclear Dilemma*, 1.

[62] Aronson, *Nuclear Weapon in the Middle East*, 74.

[63] Cohen, *Israel and the Bomb*, 44.

[64] Seymour Hersh (1991). *The Samson Option: Israel's Nuclear Arsenal and American Foreign Policy*, Tel Aviv: Yedioth Ahronoth, 34.

Francis Perrin, stated in an interview in 1986 that in 1957 France agreed to assist Israel to develop a nuclear program, with the understanding that the provided components may be used to make a bomb.[65] As part of the Israeli–French cooperation in 1958 the construction of the reactor on-site near the city of Dimona has begun. At the beginning of the construction hundreds of French scientists and technicians came to Israel, who were housed in the city of Beer Sheba.[66] In addition to contacts with the United States and France, Israel turned also to Argentina[67] and South Africa for uranium supplies[68] and Norway for heavy water supplies.[69]

The level of cooperation between Israel and South Africa increased to a level, which led to suspicions that the two countries were behind a supposedly conducted nuclear test at the event, known as the Vela incident. Vela was a powerful American satellite, which on September 22, 1979, caught two clear flashes, separated by a fraction of a second. This incident, as noted, aroused suspicion that this was a nuclear experiment. Nonetheless, a committee of nuclear experts appointed by the US administration of President Jimmy Carter, concluded that it may not be a nuclear test. This conclusion, however, did not completely remove the suspicions, and many sources question its findings.[70]

Like India and Pakistan, Israel has crossed the nuclear weaponization stage secretly, without conducting a public experiment. In fact, the uniqueness of the Israeli case study lies in the fact that Israel was the first state in the nuclear development history to complete its nuclear program without conducting a nuclear test.[71] According to the famous physicist

---

[65] Frank Barnaby (1989). *The Invisible Bomb: The Nuclear Arms Race in the Middle East*, London: I.B. Tauris, 8.

[66] Shimon Peres (1995). *Battling for Peace*, New York: Random House, 102.

[67] William Burr & Avner Cohen (2013). The Israel-Argentina Yellowcake Connection, *NSAE Briefing Book*, 432, http://nsarchive.gwu.edu/nukevault/ebb432/. Accessed 20 September 2019.

[68] Sasha Polakow-Suransky (2010). *The Unspoken Alliance*, New York: Pantheon Books, 42.

[69] Gawdat Bahgat (2008). *Proliferation of Nuclear Weapons in the Middle East*, Gainesville: University Press of Florida, 92.

[70] Jeffery Richelson (2006). The VELA Incident: Nuclear Test or Meteoroid? *NSAE Briefing Book*, 90, http://nsarchive.gwu.edu/NSAEBB/NSAEBB190/index.html. Accessed 20 September 2019.

[71] Rabinowitz, *Bargaining on Nuclear Tests*, 70.

Edward Teller, who during his visits to Israel in the late 1960s met with the senior officials of the Israeli nuclear establishment, Israel achieved a nuclear capability without conducting an experiment:

> They have it, and they were clever enough to trust their research and not to test, they knew that to test would get them into trouble.[72]

Israel's ambiguity policy, however, makes it impossible to define precisely when Israel crossed the nuclear weaponization threshold. Avner Cohen noted that on the Six-Day War eve in June 1967, Israel did not have a launchable nuclear bomb through dedicated launch platforms, such as a plane or missile, but only a nuclear device.[73] Cohen made this assessment based in his 1999 interview with Gen. (Res.) Yitzhak (Yatzhah) Cohen, who was involved in Israel's nuclear project. This assessment is also shared by other scholars.[74] Nevertheless, based on the assessments of a number of researchers, it could be assumed that the nuclear weaponization has occurred in 1968.[75]

References

Abraham, I. (1998). *The Making of the Indian Atomic Bomb*. London and New York: ZED Books.

Abraham, I. (2009). Contra-Proliferation. In Scott Sagan (Ed.), *Inside Nuclear South Asia* (pp. 106–133). Stanford, CA: Stanford University Press, 119.

Ahmed, S. (Spring 1999). Pakistan's Nuclear Weapons Program. *International Security*, 23/4, 178–204.

Aronson, S. (2014). *Nuclear Weapon in the Middle East, 1948–2013*. Jerusalem: Magnes.

Ashtana, C. & Nirmal, A. (2012). *Indian Defense: Crisis and Challenges*. Jaipur: Pointer Publishers.

[72] Cohen, *Israel and Bomb*, 298.

[73] See: *Avner Cohen's Interview* (2017, June 4). https://www.ynet.co.il/articles/0,7340,L-4971085,00.html. Accessed 20 September 2019.

[74] See for example: Jeffrey Richelson (2006). *Spying on the Bomb*, New York: W. W. Norton, 242; Bahgat, *Proliferation of Nuclear Weapons in the Middle East*, 93; Hersh, *The Samson Option*, 122.

[75] See for example: Feldman, *Nuclear Weapons and Arms Control in the Middle East*, 43; Peter Pry (1984). Israel's Nuclear Arsenal, Boulder, CO: Westview Press, 40; Shyam Bhatia (1988). *Nuclear Rivals in the Middle East*, London and New York: Routledge, 43.

Bahgat, G. (2008). *Proliferation of Nuclear Weapons in the Middle East.* Gainesville: University Press of Florida.

Barnaby, F. (1989). *The Invisible Bomb: The Nuclear Arms Race in the Middle East.* London: I.B. Tauris.

Basrur, R. (2008). *South Asia's Cold War.* London and New York: Routledge.

Ben-Gurion, D. (1975). *Behilahem Am Israel.* Tel Aviv: Am Oved [in Hebrew].

Bhatia, S. (1988). *Nuclear Rivals in the Middle East.* London and New York: Routledge.

Bidwai, P. & Vanaik, A. (2000). *New Nukes.* New York: Interlink Publishing Group, Inc.

Burr, W. (2016, May 18). National Security Archive. *Electronic Book,* 59. http://nsarchive.gwu.edu/nukevault/ebb549-INRs-NuclearWatch-1957-1967. Accessed 11 September 2011.

Burr, W. & Cohen, A. (2013). The Israel-Argentina Yellowcake Connection. *NSAE Briefing Book,* 432. http://nsarchive.gwu.edu/nukevault/ebb432/. Accessed 20 September 2019.

Carranza, M. E. (2009). *South Asian Security and International Nuclear Oder.* Farnham: Ashgate.

Chakma, B. (2010). *Pakistan's Nuclear Weapons.* London and New York: Routledge.

Chakma, B. (2011). The Pakistani Nuclear Deterrent. In Bhumitra Chakma (Ed.), The *Politics of Nuclear Weapons in South Asia* (pp. 40–53). Cornwall: TJ International.

Cheema, P. I. (2011). Nuclear and Missile Developments. In Scott Gates & Kaushik Roy (Eds.), *The Nuclear Shadow Over South Asia, 1947 to the Present* (pp. 166–177). Farnham: Ashgate.

Cheema, P. I. (2011). Nuclear and Missile Developments. In Scott Gates & Kaushik Roy (Eds.), *The Nuclear Shadow Over South Asia, 1947 to the Present* (pp. 239–250). Farnham: Ashgate, 243.

Cohen, A. (1998). *Israel and the Bomb.* New York: Columbia University Press.

Cohen, S. (2011). India as a Nuclear Power. In Scott Gates & Kaushik Roy (Eds.), *The Nuclear Shadow Over South Asia, 1947 to the Present* (pp. 159–205). Farnham: Ashgate.

Corera, G. (2006). *Shopping for Bombs.* Oxford: Oxford University Press.

Evron. (1994). *Israel's Nuclear Dilemma.* London: Routledge.

Frantz, D. & Collins, C. (2007). *The Nuclear Jihadist.* New York: Twelve.

Feldman, S. (1997). *Nuclear Weapons and Arms Control in the Middle East.* Massachusetts: Harvard University.

Ganguly, S. (2000). Explaining the Indian Nuclear Tests of 1998. In Raju Thomas & Amit Gupta (Eds.), *India's Nuclear Security* (pp. 37–66). Boulder, CO: Lynne Rienner.

Hagerty, D. (1998). *The Consequences of Nuclear Proliferation.* Cambridge: The MIT Press.

Hersh, S. (1991). *The Samson Option: Israel's Nuclear Arsenal and American Foreign Policy.* Tel Aviv: Yedioth Ahronoth.

Kapur, P. (2009). Revisionist Ambitions, Conventional Capabilities, and Nuclear Instability. Why Nuclear Asia Is Not Like Cold War Europe. In Scott Sagan (Ed.), *Inside Nuclear South Asia* (pp. 184–218). Stanford, CA: Stanford University Press.

Kerr, P. & Nikitin, M. B. (August 2016). *Pakistan's Nuclear Weapons.* Congressional Research Service.

Khalid, I. & Bano, Z. (January–June 2015). Pakistan's Nuclear Development (1974–1998): External Pressures. *South Asian Studies,* 30/1, 221–235.

Khan, F. H. (2009). Pakistan's Perspective on the Global Elimination of Nuclear Weapons. In Barry Blechman (Ed.), *Pakistan and Israel* (pp. 211–247). Washington, DC: The Henry L. Stimson Center.

Khan, F. H. (2012). *Eating Grass. The Making of the Pakistani Bomb.* Stanford: Stanford California Press.

Khan, F. H. (September 2015). Going Tactical: Pakistan's Nuclear Posture and Implications for Stability. *Proliferation Paper,* 53, 1–44.

Khan, S. (2009). *Nuclear Weapons and Conflict Transformation. The Case of India-Pakistan.* London: Routledge.

Koithara, V. (2012). *Managing India's Nuclear Forces.* Washington, DC: Brookings Institution Press.

Mian, Z. (2009). Fevered with Dreams of the Future: The Coming of the Atomic Age to Pakistan. In Itty Abraham (Ed.), *South Asian Cultures of the Bomb* (pp. 20–40). Bloomington: Indiana University Press.

Mohan, R. (1998). India and Nuclear Weapons. *Internationale Politik und Geselschaft,* 4, 377–383.

Pandey, N. N. & Chakma, B. (2011). Nuclear Proliferation in South Asia and Its Impact on Regional Cooperation. In Bhumitra Chakma (Ed.), *The Politics of Nuclear Weapons in South Asia* (pp. 137–154). Farnham: Ashgate.

Paul, T. V. (2002). India, the International System and Nuclear Weapons. In Damodar Sardesai & Raju Thomas (Eds.), *Nuclear India in the Twenty First Century* (pp. 85–104). New York: Palgrave Macmillan.

Peres, S. (1995). *Battling for Peace.* New York: Random House.

Perkovich, G. (1999). *India's Nuclear Bomb.* Los Angeles: University of California Press.

Perkovich, G. (2002). What Makes the Indian Bomb Tick? In Damodar Sardesai & Raju Thomas (Eds.), *Nuclear India in the Twenty First Century* (pp. 25–60). New York: Palgrave Macmillan.

Polakow-Suransky, S. (2010). *The Unspoken Alliance.* New York: Pantheon Books.

Pry, P. (1984). *Israel's Nuclear Arsenal.* Boulder, CO: Westview Press.

Rabinowitz, O. (2014). *Bargaining on Nuclear Tests: Washington and Its Cold War Deals.* Oxford: Oxford University Press.

Rajain, A. (2005). *Nuclear Deterrence in Southern Asia*. New Delhi: Sage.

Raz, A. (2015). *Hamaavak al Hapzaza*. Jerusalem: Carmel [in Hebrew].

Reed, T. & Stillman, D. (2009). *The Nuclear Express*. Minnesota: Zenith Press.

ur-Rehman, S. (1999). *Long Road to Chagai*. Islamabad: Print Wise Publication.

Richelson, J. (2006). *Spying on the Bomb*. New York: W. W. Norton.

Richelson, J. (2006). The VELA Incident: Nuclear Test or Meteoroid? *NSAE Briefing Book*, 90. http://nsarchive.gwu.edu/NSAEBB/NSAEBB190/index. html. Accessed 20 September 2019.

Shalom, Z. (2005). *Israel's Nuclear Option*. Portland and Tel Aviv: Sussex Academic Press and JCSS.

Spector, L. (1988). *The Undeclared Bomb*. Cambridge, MA: Ballinger Publishing Company.

Subrahmanyan, K. (2002). India and the International Nuclear Order. In Damodar Sardesai & Raju Thomas (Eds.), *Nuclear India in the Twenty First Century* (pp. 63–84). New York: Palgrave Macmillan.

Zarah, F. (2000). Pakistan's Elusive Search for Nuclear Parity with India. In Raju Thomas & Amit Gupta (Eds.), *India's Nuclear Security* (pp. 145–170). Boulder, CO: Lynne Rienner.

Avner Cohen's Interview. (2017, June 4). https://www.ynet.co.il/articles/0,7340, L-4971085,00.html. Accessed 20 September 2019.

Jawaharlal Nehru's Speeches, September 1957–April 1963. (1964). New Delhi: Ministry of Information and Broadcasting.

Nuclear Chronology 1970–1974. http://www.bhutto.org/article21.php. Accessed 11 September 2019.

Vielleict Sind Wiir Naiv, Idioten Sind Wir Nicht. (2011, June 27). *Der Spiegel*. http://m.spiegel.de/politik/ausland/pakistans-atombombe-vielleicht-sind-wir-naiv-idioten-sind-wir-nicht-a-770498.html. Accessed 5 September 2019 [in German].

CHAPTER 6

The Nuclear Weaponization and the Patterns of Conventional Warfighting

Abstract This chapter is dedicated to an empirical examination of the nuclear weaponization influence on the patterns of warfighting of India, Pakistan, and Israel at the conventional battlefield. In order to explore such influence, we first examine the patterns of conventional warfighting that were practically implemented by Pakistan, India, and Israel in the pre-weaponization period. Subsequently, we explore the nuclear weaponization influence on the countries' warfighting patterns during conventional conflicts. Accordingly, the discussion in each case study is divided into two periods—before and after crossing the nuclear weaponization threshold.

Keywords Defense and restraint · First strike · First use nuclear policy · Offensive and escalation · "Weak-Strong Actors Paradox"

In Chapter 3 we attributed the specific models of nuclear weaponization influence to each examined country. This chapter will be dedicated to an empirical examination of the weaponization influence on the patterns of warfighting of India, Pakistan, and Israel on the conventional battlefield. In order to explore such influence, we first examine the patterns of conventional warfighting, as were practically implemented by Pakistan, India, and Israel in pre-weaponization period. Subsequently, we explore

© The Author(s) 2020
I. Davidzon, *Patterns of Conventional*
Warfighting under the Nuclear Umbrella,
https://doi.org/10.1007/978-3-030-45594-1_6

the nuclear weaponization influence on the countries' warfighting patterns during the conventional conflicts.

Accordingly, the discussion in each case study will be divided into two periods—before and after crossing the nuclear weaponization threshold. As abovementioned, Pakistan and India crossed weaponization threshold in 1987 and 1990, respectively. Therefore, chronologically both countries fought three conventional wars against each other in the pre-weaponization period—in 1947, 1965, and 1971. Therefore, the Kargil war that took place in 1999, is the last conventional war to date in the hostility's history of India and Pakistan.

As for Israel, in view of the fact that the country crossed the weaponization threshold in 1968, after the Six-Day War, we can conclude that three wars belong chronologically to pre-weaponization period: Independence war in 1948, Sinai war in 1956, and the Six-Day War in 1967. Accordingly, to date the first and last conventional war that took place in the post-weaponization period was the Yom Kippur war in October 1973.

PAKISTAN AND INDIA: *AGGRESSION ENCOURAGEMENT* VS. *RESTRAINT IMPOSITION*

Pre-weaponization Period

First Indo-Pak War

The first war between the two countries took place almost immediately after both declared their independence.[1] As abovementioned, the background to the war was the refusal of the local ruler of Kashmir, Maharaja Hari Singh, to join one of the new states and his hope to establish his own independent country.[2] The escalation began in August 1947 in the village of Nila Bat, as a demonstration, which was held by Muslims demanding the entry of Kashmir into Pakistan, was forcibly dispersed by the local forces of the Kashmiri government.[3] On October 3, the representatives of the pro-Pakistani rebel forces announced in the Pakistani

---

[1] Ganguli, *The Origins of War in South Asia*, 17.

[2] Ganguly & Kapur, *India, Pakistan, and the Bomb*, 10–11.

[3] Nawaz, *Crossed Swords*, 43.

city of Rawalpindi a temporary government of the Jammu and Kashmir region.[4] Pakistanis have mobilized tribal forces, *lashkars*, to conquer Kashmir and annex it to their country. It was the first use of irregular forces, militia, as a prelude to the conventional war.[5] On October 22, 1947, irregular Pakistani troops invaded Kashmir.[6]

Arjun Subramaniam noted in his book "India's Wars" that the invasion of the pro-Pakistani forces was actually part of the Gulmarg plan led by a senior Pakistan Army officer:

> It was there that a group of hard-core Islamist Muslim officers led by Colonel Akbar Khan in collusion with the future leadership of Pakistan regularly met at Jinnah's residence at Aurangzeb Road and put together an audacious plan to seize the princely state of Jammu and Kashmir through armed action...[7]

According to the plan, the aim was to force the Kashmir's ruler to join Pakistan through an invasion of Pakistani irregular forces from the tribal areas in Pakistan. If necessary, the Pakistan military will then join the fighting to complete the mission.[8]

The Pakistani invasion advanced toward Kashmir Valley along the Muzaffarabad–Srinagar road.[9] Already on October 23, armed tribesmen, under the command of a Pakistani commander, occupied the first city in Kashmir–Muzaffarabad.[10] The invaders began to advance toward the city of Srinagar, the seat of the Kashmiri ruler. On October 26, without significant resistance from local defense forces, was captured the city

---

[4] Sumantra Bose (2003). *Kashmir: Roots of Conflict, Paths to Peace*, Cambridge and London: Harvard University Press, 33.

[5] Jones & Fair, *Counterinsurgency in Pakistan*, 7.

[6] Mushtaq Ahmad Mir (April 2014). India-Pakistan: The History of Unsolved Conflicts, *IOSR, Journal of Humanities and Social Science*, 19/4, 105.

[7] Arjun Subramaniam (2016). *India's Wars: A Military History 1947–1971*, Noida: HarperCollins Publishers India, 113.

[8] Subramaniam, *India's Wars*, 113–114.

[9] Subramaniam, *India's Wars*, 199.

[10] Agha Humayun Amin (1999). *The 1947–48 Kashmir War: The War of Lost Opportunities*, Lahore: Strategicus and Tacticus, https://archive.org/stream/The1947-48KashmirWarTheWarOfLostOpportunities/49202996-The-1947-48-Kashmir-War-Revised_djvu.txt. Accessed 26 October 2019.

of Baramulla.[11] In light of the military successes of the Pakistani forces, Maharaja urgently requested on October 24 India to provide military aid to repel the invasion.[12] Upon the Kashmiri government consent to join India, the Indian Prime Minister Nehru agreed to intervene in the conflict and send military forces to stop the Pakistani attack.[13] As part of the first operation of the Indian forces, Operation Jak, conducted on October 27, 1947, Indian forces took over Srinagar airport.[14] First, the Indian army acted to prevent Srinagar from falling into the hands of the enemy. Later, however, the Indians took the initiative and moved on to the offensive phase, pushing Pakistanis from around Srinagar and its airport.[15] The Indian offensive advanced and even gained momentum for the conquest of the city of Muzaffarabad, but eventually stopped.[16] Notwithstanding the successes from December 1947 the Indian Army suffered logistical problems, which made it difficult to continue the offensive.[17] It should be noted, that the hostilities took place in other areas as well—to the north and northeast of the Kashmir valley and to the south of the valley. In the winter of 1948, the Indian Command was forming forces to decide the war, even at the expense of an escalation and opening another front in Punjab.[18] In the spring of that year, the fighting resumed, the Indian Army continued to advance to the depths of Kashmir and expanded territory, which will eventually be a part of the Indian Kashmir.[19]

As aforementioned, an invasion of irregular tribal forces turned into an invasion of regular Pakistani military forces. Upon the entry of the Indian Army to Kashmir and its successful operations at the battlefield, in the spring of 1948 the Pakistani strategy evolved from the unofficial

[11] Subramaniam, *India's Wars*, 120.

[12] Bose, *Kashmir: Roots of Conflict, Paths to Peace*, 35.

[13] Ganguly & Kapur, *India, Pakistan, and the Bomb*, 11.

[14] Rohit Singh (Autumn 2012). Operations in Jammu and Kashmir 1947–48, *Scholar Warrior*, 137.

[15] Bose, *Kashmir: Roots of Conflict, Paths to Peace*, 37.

[16] Russel Brines (1968). *The Indo-Pakistani Conflict*, London: Pall Mall Press, 71.

[17] Bhashyam Kasturi (2008). The State of War with Pakistan, in Daniel Martson & Chandar Sundaram (Eds.), *A Military History of India and South Asia*, Bloomington and Indianapolis: Indiana University Press, 142.

[18] Subramaniam, *India's Wars*, 155.

[19] Bose, *Kashmir: Roots of Conflict, Paths to Peace*, 40–41.

support of tribal forces into an open involvement of the Pakistani military in the conflict.[20] The aim of the military was to prevent the collapse of the tribal militants, or as they are commonly called in Pakistan *Azad Forces*, i.e., the freedom fighters.[21] At the final phase of the war, the Pakistani army conducted an offensive operation from the mountainous areas of Kashmir toward the north.[22] This attack, however, was suppressed on November 1, 1948 in the Sojila Pass area by the Indian forces, which took over territories in the Ladakh area (the Buddhist region in Kashmir), that eventually enabled the establishment of a strategic highway between Srinagar and Leh (a central town in Ladach).[23]

Eventually after the UN mediation, the war ended on January 1, 1949, with the cease-fire. At the end of the war, Pakistan and India gained control over one-third and two-thirds of the territory of Kashmir, respectively.[24]

As far as the Pakistani military is concerned, the first confrontation with the Indian army was reflected in the first implementation of its warfighting pattern: a tendency to initiate and escalate the confrontations; a two-stage strategy evolving from the use of irregular forces to the direct involvement of the Pakistani regular armed forces in a war. Although this war didn't solve the Kashmir dispute, it demonstrated the effectiveness of irregular forces supported unofficially by Islamabad as a tool to challenge India. Given the Pakistani perception of New Delhi as a powerful enemy, the adoption by Pakistan of such a strategy was designated to minimize the use of regular armed forces.[25] Such a strategy was designated to minimize the possibility of deterioration to the open war and probable defeat of Pakistan's military.[26]

Regarding India, the pattern of warfighting of its military during the first war reflected its conduct in other wars in the pre-weaponization period: India, as part of the status quo state perception, demonstrated

[20] Kapur & Ganguly, The Jihad Paradox, 119.

[21] Nawaz, *Crossed Swords*, 67.

[22] Bose, *Kashmir: Roots of Conflict, Paths to Peace*, 41.

[23] Kasturi, The State of War with Pakistan, 142.

[24] Kapur & Ganguly, The Jihad Paradox, 119.

[25] Paul Kapur & Sumit Ganguly (Summer 2012). The Jihad Paradox: Pakistan and Islamist Militancy in South Asia, *International Security*, 37/1, 118.

[26] Kapur & Ganguly, The Jihad Paradox, 119–120.

restraint, didn't initiate the hostilities, but just reacted to the Pakistani escalation. Moreover, the Indians, as part of their irreconcilable attitude regarding any threat to their territories or interests, were even considering to escalate the conflict by expanding the geographic scope of the combat zone to Punjab area. Nevertheless, such a plan was not implemented presumably due to international efforts to bring the conflict to an end by diplomatic means.

Second Indo-Pak War

The next war between India and Pakistan occurred in 1965. This war was preceded by escalation and fighting in April between India and Pakistan in the Rann of Kutch area, a sparsely populated area along the Indo-Pakistani border.[27] From Islamabad's point of view, this confrontation was relatively successful. Thus, in the first encounter on April 10, Indians suffered casualties and the battle resulted in military defeat of the Indian armed forces.[28]

Altaf Gauhar, the Minister of Communications in Ayub Khan's government at the time, noted the uplifting mood prevailing at the General Staff in light of the success of the Pakistani military during the fighting:

> The brigadiers and colonels were all excited about the way the Indians had abounded their positions and retreated in total disarray. Now was the opportunity to pursue the enemy deep into his territory.[29]

The satisfaction of the Pakistani senior officer with the results of the confrontation in Rann of Kuch eventually led a few months later to a decision to initiate a war against India. It was assumed, that Pakistan could cut off Kashmir from India and defeat the Indian army, just as it happened in the Rann of Kutch.[30] Subsequently, the Pakistani army drafted the war plan for the liberation of Kashmir, dubbed "Gibraltar Operation",[31] named after Tariq ibn Ziyad, which led the conquest

---

[27] Kasturi, The State of War with Pakistan, 143.

[28] Lubnan Abid Ali (July–December 2009). The Rann of Kutch and Its Aftermath, *A Research Journal of South Asian Studies*, 24/2, 252.

[29] Gauhar, *Ayub Khan*, 199.

[30] Gauhar, *Ayub Khan*, 209.

[31] Subramaniam, *India's Wars*, 275.

of Spain in 711.[32] The Pakistani warfighting pattern was the same as in the first Indo-Pak war.[33] As part of the first phase of this operation, on August 5, 1965, Pakistan sent infiltrators into Indian Kashmir.[34] The purpose of this phase was to provoke a local uprising in Kashmir that would free the region from the rule of India.[35] The invaders were divided into five groups, named after Muslim warlords: Tariq, Qasim, Khalid, Salahuddin and Ghaznavi.[36] Despite the expectation that subversion and sabotage actions will bring about the local population revolt, it hasn't occurred.[37] The majority of the armed groups' members were discovered by Indian forces, in some cases with the assistance of the local residents themselves. The invaders haven't benefited from the climate conditions. Thus, for instance, the Tariq group, failed to adapt itself to the Himalayan climate. In fact, only the Ghaznavi group managed to hold on, retaining control over some areas in the west and southwest Jammu region, and did not retreat until the cease-fire.[38] Despite the loss of tactical surprise, Pakistan continued fighting and even escalated it by sending regular troops across the armistice line near the city of Bhimbar in Azad Kashmir territory. In response, Indian forces have also crossed the armistice line.[39] The Indian offensive was aimed at the bases, from which the militants infiltrated into the Indian territory.[40] In response to such an attack, Pakistan once again escalated the fighting and opened another front in Punjab area under Operation Grand Slam. Then, on August 31 and September 1, the Pakistani army conducted an artillery aid armored attack in southern Kashmir to cut off the Jammu and Kashmir region from the rest of India.[41]

It should be emphasized that at the basis of the operational plan of the Pakistan military before the war was the assumption that, like the

---

[32] Jones & Fair, *Counterinsurgency in Pakistan*, 9.

[33] Ganguly & Kapur, *India, Pakistan, and the Bomb*, 12.

[34] Subramaniam, *India's Wars*, 277.

[35] Jones & Fair, *Counterinsurgency in Pakistan*, 10.

[36] Gauhar, *Ayub Khan*, 212.

[37] Ganguli & Hagerty, *Fearful Symmetry*, 29.

[38] Gauhar, *Ayub Khan*, 212–213.

[39] Ganguli & Hagerty, *Fearful Symmetry*, 29.

[40] Kasturi, The State of War with Pakistan, 144.

[41] Subramaniam, *India's Wars*, 282.

first round of war in 1947–1948, this time the Indian military would not extend the fighting beyond the Kashmir region.[42] This expectation, however, did not materialize, as the Indians realized that the conditions at the area did not allow effective defense organization, took initiative and escalated the fighting while opening a second front in Punjab. This step matched the traditional pattern of Indian military operation—a tendency to escalate a conflict after the start of hostilities, mainly by expanding the geographic scope of the combat zone. On September 6, 1965, the Indian forces crossed the international border and attacked not far from the Pakistani city of Lahore.[43] Later, the Prime Minister of India at the time, Shastri, explained the rationale of the Indian attack toward Lahore in response to Pakistan's previous offensive move:

> [It] was no border incident, and they [Pakistani forces] crossed not only the cease-fire line but also the international border and entered the Chhamb territory of Jammu. Time was of the essence and we had to act quickly. Although Pakistan's attack was first launched in Chhamb, they had an eye on our territory of Punjab also. As you know, they made a rocket attack on Amritsar and tried to destroy the airport near Wagah.[44]

The attack in the direction of Lahore also assisted in defense of Kashmir, forcing the Pakistanis to split their efforts to protect the territories in Punjab.[45]

Additional offensive effort directed to the city of Sialkot.[46] While the attack on Lahore was relatively successful, during which the Indian army conquered several villages in its vicinity, the advance toward Sialkot ended in failure: the Indian forces have not reached the target due to the destroyed bridges over the water channel connecting the city by the Pakistanis.[47] Consistent with the strategic culture perception of India as an existential threat to Pakistan, the Indian escalation was viewed by the Pakistani leadership as a war for the very existence of the Muslim state.

---

[42] Alastair Lamb (1991). *Kashmir: A Disputed Legacy*, Hertfordshire: Roxford Books, 260.

[43] Ganguli & Hagerty, *Fearful Symmetry*, 30.

[44] Brines, *The Indo-Pakistani Conflict*, 330.

[45] Ganguli & Hagerty, *Fearful Symmetry*, 30.

[46] Lamb, *Kashmir: A Disputed Legacy*, 262.

[47] Brines, *The Indo-Pakistani Conflict*, 338.

During the fighting, the President of Pakistan Ayub Khan stated in his speech to the nation:

> We are at the war... Our soldiers have gone forward to repel the enemy... The Indian rulers were never reconciled to the establishment of an independent Pakistan homeland of our own. All their military preparations during the past eighteen years have been against us... We always knew these arms would be raised against us. Time has proved this so.[48]

To ease the pressure in the Lahore and Sialkot region, Pakistan's forces launched a counteroffensive on September 7 in the Indian part of Punjab, toward the city of Amritsar, which is located east of Lahore.[49] Despite the relative success of the Pakistani forces, no breakthrough was recorded at the front and both armies fought defensive battles.[50] Toward the middle of September 1965 against the backdrop of a Stagnation at the front, both adversaries were under pressure to reach a cease-fire. Consequently, on September 21 and 22, India and Pakistan declared the cease-fire, respectively.[51] Upon the end of hostilities, both foes retreated to the cease-fire lines before August 1965. In January 1966, the leaders of both countries met in Tashkent (which then was part of the former Soviet Union) and signed an agreement whereby they undertook to continue negotiations and honor the cease-fire.[52]

It is worth noting that during the second Indo-Pak war, the eastern part of Pakistan remained out of combat and was in fact not included in Pakistan's military war plans. According to the Pakistani command's approach, the protection of the eastern part of the country was dependent upon the protection of the western part. Therefore, most of the forces were concentrated in the west, thus exposing the eastern part to the Indian military threat. This decision will contribute, *inter alia*, to the formation of a fertile land of dissatisfaction in East Pakistan from the dominance of the western part of the country, which will evolve into

---

[48] Brines, *The Indo-Pakistani Conflict*, 334.

[49] Gauhar, *Ayub Khan*, 225.

[50] Brines, *The Indo-Pakistani Conflict*, 338–342.

[51] Ganguli & Hagerty, *Fearful Symmetry*, 30.

[52] Kasturi, The State of War with Pakistan, 144.

the civil war and further deterioration into the third Indo-Pak war, also known as the Bangladesh war.[53]

Third Indo-Pak War

The third Indo-Pakistan war was different from the two previous wars, since it didn't originate from the dispute over Kashmir but rather from the domestic political process within Pakistan. In 1970–1971, internal tensions in Pakistani society increased. The split between the western part, with the dominance of the Punjabi and Pashtuns population, and the eastern part of the Bengal part of the state, deepened the rift within the country.[54]

In the free elections held in December 1970, the Awami League party led by the East Pakistani Sheikh Mujibur Rahman won 160 out of 162 seats in parliament while the PPP (Pakistan People's Party) led by Zulfikar Ali Bhutto won only 81 seats in the west. This gave Awami League a majority in the parliament and the ability to form a government.[55] The results of the election brought both political forces into conflict. Months of discussions conducted between Bhutto and Rahman in an attempt to reach a compromise did not yield results and finally failed in March 1971.[56] Immediately after the failure of the discussions, the Pakistani army began to take an uncompromising position against the Bengali opposition forces in the east, which caused an influx of refugees to the West Bengal region of India.[57] Under such circumstances, the flow of thousands of refugees into India could also create instability therein. On March 25, 1971, the Pakistani armed forces began to disarm the East Pakistani resistance force. *Mukti Bahini*, who supported the opposition and received logistic assistance from India. India's support did not hinder the Pakistani military from continuing the repression. Additionally, Pakistani forces suppressed protests in Dhaka and arrested the leader of Awami League, Sheikh Mujibur Rahman.[58]

The internal tensions in Pakistan quickly escalated to the war with India. Although, as mentioned above, New Delhi has been already

---

[53] Ganguly & Kapur, *India, Pakistan, and the Bomb*, 14.

[54] Subramaniam, *India's Wars*, 338.

[55] Khan, *Eating Grass*, 74.

[56] Subramaniam, *India's Wars*, 338.

[57] Kasturi, The State of War with Pakistan, 146.

[58] Khan, Eating Grass, 75.

involved in the political crisis of Pakistan, however, during November–December limited fighting took place at the border area between Pakistani, Indian and *Mukti Bahini* forces.[59]

Under such circumstances and in line with its traditional warfighting pattern, Islamabad chose to escalate the conflict. The third conventional war between India and Pakistan began on December 3, 1971, with the Pakistan Air Force attack on India's military bases, in the north-western part of the state.[60] The next day, in response to the air attack, the India Air Force retaliated.[61] According to their warfighting pattern, the Indian military escalated the conflict on the commencement of hostilities. It expanded geographically by deployment of its naval force. As Bhashyam Kasturi noted, it was "the first full-scale Indian naval war".[62] Along with blockading the East Pakistani coast, India's naval forces attacked oil installations in Karachi harbor. On the ground, the Indian forces, with the assistance of the Bengal guerrillas, invaded East Pakistan and began to advance toward the capital of eastern Pakistan, the city of city Dhaka. The fighting also took place in the west, with Pakistani operations in Kashmir and Punjab. India retaliated there again by geographically expanding the combat zone through the offensive operation toward Pakistani territory, at the Sialkot–Shakargarh area.[63]

On December 15, 1971, the Indian army launched a final attack on the capital of East Pakistan and the following day Pakistani commander, General Niazi, agreed to cease fire and surrender.[64]

This conventional war was the last one in the pre-weaponization period. As we have seen, during this period the armed forces of both, India and Pakistan, were operating at the battlefield according to their fighting patterns. It will be almost thirty years later and relations between the two countries will deteriorate again into a war—this time after both have obtained nuclear weapons.

---

[59] Lachhman Singh (1979). *Indian Sword Strikes in East Pakistan*, Ghaziabad: Vikas Publishing, 23–30.

[60] Ganguli (1986). *The Origins of War in South Asia*, 97.

[61] Kasturi, The State of War with Pakistan, 146.

[62] Kasturi, The State of War with Pakistan, 148.

[63] Kasturi, The State of War with Pakistan, 147.

[64] Khan, Eating Grass, 77.

Post-weaponization Period

The Kargil war is the fourth war fought by India and Pakistan since their independence. The war was preceded by the infiltration of Pakistani forces at the end of 1998 across the Kashmir border (LoC) and the subsequent capture of 12-kilometer positions in Indian territory.[65] These positions topographically dominated the area between the border line and the Srinagar–Kargil–Leh road.[66] This road was a supply route for Indian troops deployed in the Siachin glacier, which was seized by the Indian Army after the fighting over the area with the Pakistanis in 1984.[67]

Toward the end of April 1999, the Pakistanis established about 100 positions to prevent the Indian army from crossing the border into the Pakistani Kashmir region.

It should be emphasized that the infiltration of Pakistani forces into Indian territory was performed secretly. At first, Indians believed it was a limited infiltration.[68] On May 19, 1999 at a press conference in Srinagar, a senior Indian officer stated that it was a local infiltration backed by the Pakistani military, which would be treated accordingly.[69] Moreover, pursuant to General Malik, Pakistani aggression was actually a surprise for New Delhi:

> The Kargil Review Committee had evidence that the Pakistani armed intrusion in the Kargil sector came as a complete surprise to the Indian government, Army and intelligence agencies as the J&K government and its agencies. There was no agency or individual who had been able to realize before the event the possibility of such a large -scale Pakistani military intrusion.[70]

Nevertheless, the Indians soon realized that it was not a local, limited situation.[71] After the discovery of the Pakistani invasion, at the end of

---

[65] Kapur, Ten Years of Instability in a Nuclear South Asia, 73.

[66] Malik (2006). *Kargil: From Surprise to Victory*, 2.

[67] Khan, *Eating Grass*, 309.

[68] Mubeen Adnan (2015). The Kargil Crisis and Pakistan's Constraints, *Journal of Political Studies*, 22/1, 135.

[69] Malik, *India's Military Conflicts and Diplomacy*, 247.

[70] Malik, *India's Military Conflicts and Diplomacy*, 245.

[71] Khan, *Eating Grass*, 311.

May, the Indian army began to move forces to Kargil. Since most of the Indian army offensive units were deployed at depths of the country, far from the border with Pakistan, it took the Indians close to three weeks to concentrate forces at Kargil to begin a military operation.[72] The Indian reaction to the Pakistani infiltration and the occupation of the positions in Indian territory was performed in the framework of the Vijay operation.[73] The operation, which started in May, wasn't successful at the beginning, partially due to the topographical conditions—Indian soldiers had to climb mountains to capture fortified enemy positions. In order to recapture the positions, the Indian forces had to fight hard and long battles. Thus, for instance, the Tololing position, which is situated less than 5 kilometers from Dras town on the Srinagar–Kargil–Leh road, was captured only on 17 June, after approximately three weeks of fighting.[74] Jubar Ridge, which is located several kilometers from the LoC, was recaptured on July 8, after a fierce battle that lasted for 40 days.[75] Finally, after the harsh fighting, the Indian army took over all of the occupied positions.[76] The war ended in mid-July 1999 upon the complete withdrawal of the Pakistanis from the Indian territory.[77]

So far, we have briefly reviewed the Kargil War. Is it possible to detect a change in the way the war was managed by the Indian and Pakistani armies as a result of the introduction of the nuclear weaponization? According to our assumption, in the interstate conflict, with the mutual possession of nuclear weapon, a weaker country, with the perception of power inferiority *vis-à-vis* enemy and/or revisionist beliefs, will perceive a nuclear arsenal as a shield against a superior conventional capability of an adversary. In this case, nuclear weapon is expected to encourage aggression. Indeed, the conduct of the Pakistani military during the Kargil War resembles the *Aggression Encouragement* model of nuclear weaponization influence. As a weaker state *vis-à-vis* India, Pakistan perceived an acquisition of nuclear weapon as a change of relative power. In other words, Pakistanis treat the nuclear weapon as a kind of "force

---

[72] Walter Ludwig (2015). Indian Military Modernization and Conventional Deterrence in South Asia, *The Journal of Strategic Studies*, 38/5, 2015, 745–746.

[73] Malik, *India's Military Conflicts and Diplomacy*, 1.

[74] Malik, *Kargil: From Surprise to Victory*, Chapter 8.

[75] Kasturi, The State of War with Pakistan, 150.

[76] Kasturi, The State of War with Pakistan, 149.

[77] Ganguli & Hagerty, *Fearful Symmetry*, 157.

multiplier" or, in a certain sense, force equalizer, which allowed the Pakistani forces to act during the war in 1999 as in previous wars in 1947, 1965 and 1971. The nuclear weaponization enabled to proceed with the same pattern of conventional warfighting, which derived from the strategic culture rooted perception of inferiority and revisionist beliefs regarding the Kargil dispute. Thus, the Pakistani army could follow its warfighting pattern, without fear from the opponent's conventional superiority. Moreover, according to Bruce Riedel, a former CIA analyst, during Kargil war the American intelligence warned the American President at the time, Bill Clinton, that Pakistan could use the nuclear weapon during the war:

> The morning of the Fourth (of July, 1999), the CIA wrote in its top-secret Daily Brief that Pakistan was preparing its nuclear weapons for deployment and possible use. The intelligence was very compelling.[78]

In line with its perception of nuclear weapon as a shield against India's superior conventional capabilities, Pakistan refused to declare a commitment to a no first use policy regarding its nuclear arsenal.[79] In January 2002, General Lieutenant Kidwai the head of Strategic Plans Division in the Pakistani military, listed a number of scenarios in which Pakistan will use the nuclear weapon:

- India attacks Pakistan and conquers a large part of its territory (space threshold)
- India destroys a large part either of its land or air forces (military threshold)
- India proceeds to the economic strangling of Pakistan (economic strangling)

---

[78] "Pakistan was to Deploy Nukes Against India During Kargil War" (2018, July 12), https://economictimes.indiatimes.com/news/defence/pakistan-was-to-deploy-nukes-against-india-during-kargil-war/articleshow/50019153.cms?from=mdr. Accessed 12 November 2019.

[79] Sadia Tasleem (2016, June 30). Pakistan's Nuclear Use Doctrine, https://carnegieendowment.org/2016/06/30/pakistan-s-nuclear-use-doctrine-pub-63913. Accessed 12 November 2019.

- India pushes Pakistan into political destabilization or creates a large-scale internal subversion in Pakistan (domestic destabilization).[80]

This declaratory policy is formulated deliberately ambiguously to deter conventional and nuclear attack as well.[81] Despite the vague formulation, the key feature of Islamabad's nuclear doctrine is that Pakistan will use the nuclear weapon once its conventional forces would not be able to deter an Indian attack or to prevent a conquest of significant part of its territory.[82] According to Feroz Hassan Khan, the Pakistani posture is similar to that of NATO during the Cold War:

> There are [in Pakistan] geographic gaps and corridors similar to those that existed in Europe (such as erstwhile "Fulda gap") that are vulnerably to exploitation by mechanized Indian troops. In general, the situation as is it was with East and West Germany. With its relative smaller conventional force, and lacking adequate technical means, especially in early warning and surveillance, Pakistan relies on a more proactive nuclear defense policy.[83]

During the Cold War, in view of the Soviet military's quantitative superiority, the North-Atlantic alliance adopted a similar nuclear doctrine. Despite such similarities between both cases, the case of Pakistan is different, in the sense that this strategy is used by Islamabad to challenge the status quo rather than maintaining it.

Consequently, Islamabad initiated the war and as before, it commenced through the use of irregular forces. The official version in Pakistan was that the escalation in Kargil area began with the infiltration of guerrillas, the Mujahideen (freedom fighters), without the involvement of the Pakistan's army. Thus, for example, Pervez Musharraf, Pakistani army Chief of Staff during the Kargil War, argued:

[80] Report on Nuclear Safety, Nuclear Stability and Nuclear Strategy in Pakistan (2002, January 14), https://pugwash.org/2002/01/14/report-on-nuclear-safety-nuclear-stability-and-nuclear-strategy-in-pakistan/. Accessed 12 November 2019.

[81] Khan, Challenges to Nuclear Stability in South Asia, 65.

[82] Narang, *Nuclear Strategy in The Modern Era*, 80.

[83] Khan, Challenges to Nuclear Stability in South Asia, 65.

> We knew the thousands of mujahideen (freedom fighters), mostly indigenous to the Indian-held Kashmir but also supported by freelance sympathizers from Pakistan, did operate again the Indian forces. They used to cross the Line of Control (LoC) in both directions at places which were thinly held and were the going was rough.[84]

According to Musharraf, the infiltration activity was allegedly completely independent and only became known to the Pakistani Command in retrospect. Nevertheless, after becoming aware of the infiltration, the Pakistani military decided to escalate the confrontation by deployment of regular armed forces to take advantage of the situation on the ground and capture the positions previously taken by the militants to strengthen them against an expected Indian attack.

Contrary to this description of events, General Malik, Indian Army Chief of Staff at the time, claimed that the outbreak of the war was preceded by a strict planning process of the Pakistan army:

> ...the Pakistan Army – a state within a state- was busy planning and carrying out reconnaissance to initiate intrusion in the Kargil sector. Operation "Badr" as it was called, was to be launched by 10 Corps of Pakistani Army.[85]

According to this version, the entire operation was carried out by regular armed forces, without militias' involvement.[86] In any case, it is evident that the Pakistani army adopted an old pattern of using infiltrators from tribal groups or military men disguised as tribesmen, as a prelude to the entry of the regular army into the war.

In view of the foregoing, the acquired nuclear umbrella encouraged a relatively aggressive and offensive pattern of conventional warfighting, as it was implemented by the Pakistani army over the years in pre-weaponization period. It allowed the Pakistani military to fight according to the preferred pattern of warfighting, consistent with the strategic culture of country: initiation and escalation of war through the two-stage strategy of a combined use of irregular forces or regular forces disguised as tribesmen, as a prelude to transition to a phase of

---

[84] Musharraf, *In the Line of Fire*, 88.

[85] Malik, *India's Military Conflicts and Diplomacy*, 240.

[86] Christine Fair (2019). Militants in the Kargil Conflict: Myths, Realities, and Impacts, in Peter Lavoy (Ed.), *Asymmetric Warfare in South Asia*, Cambridge University Press, 233.

conventional warfare, involving the participation of the regular forces. In other words, based on the strategic culture perception of the pre-existing strategic threat of Pakistani decision-makers regarding their conventional military inferiority and the image of enemy, Pakistan adopted the first use nuclear policy to be able to fight according to its traditional escalation and an offensive warfighting pattern.

As for the Indian military, the nuclear weaponization effect on its conduct was different. Pursuant to the assumption regarding the influence of nuclear weaponization, the stronger in conventional terms state *vis-à-vis* its nuclear-armed adversary, will perceive an introduction of a nuclear weapon into the conflict as a restraining factor. Such an effect causes the "Weak-Strong Actors Paradox", pursuant to which the weaker side gets a relative advantage over the strong side. In other words, superior capabilities of a stronger country are offset by a nuclear weapon of a weaker opponent. Therefore, a nuclear weaponization caused change in the opposite direction—instead of encouraging aggression it imposed restraint.

Regarding the conduct of the Indian military, Sumit Ganguly and David Haggerty argued, that possession of nuclear weapons by both sides has had an impact on New Delhi's readiness to escalate the conflict and to expand it geographically:

> In effect, the mutual possession of nuclear weapons was the critical determinant in controlling both vertical and horizontal escalation. The Indian politico-military elite was now acutely cognizant of Pakistan's status as an overt nuclear weapons state, and therefore realized it would act with considerable restraint.[87]

On the one hand, India did not initiate the war but merely reacted to the Pakistani invasion—which corresponds to the first characteristic of the Indian warfighting pattern. On the other hand, it refrained from geographically expanding the conflict and transferring combat activities to Pakistan's territory.

According to General Malik, the nuclear weapon dimension played a role in India's decision-making during Kargil war.[88] The issue of Indian response to the Pakistani invasion was debated at the meeting headed by

---

[87] Ganguli & Hagerty, *Fearful Symmetry*, 161.
[88] Malik, *Kargil: From Surprise to Victory*, 253.

the Prime Minister of India on May 18, and the military was requested not to cross the international border with Pakistan. Malik also noted:

> The next day, 25 May 1999, Prime Minister Vajpayee declared that the new situation was not infiltration but a move to occupy Indian territory. He said that "all steps will be taken to clear the Kargil area." He also declared that Indian troops would not cross the LoC [Line of Control].[89]

It should be noted, that the Indian Air force received the same instruction. As General Malik stated:

> The Air Force joined in the offensive actions against the Pak intruders after political clearance was given on 24 May with the proviso that the LoC should not be crossed.[90]

It should be emphasized, that certain senior Indian politicians, such as the former Indian National Security Adviser Brajesh Mishra and Defense Minister George Fernandes, argued ex post, that if necessary, the government would consider ordering the military to cross the border, regardless of the Pakistani nuclear threat.[91] Nevertheless, an examination of the practical behavior of the Indian military demonstrates a change in the pattern of warfighting compared to the pre-weaponization period.

Moreover, an analysis the of the Indian military's warfighting pattern reveals another element, which was absent during the Kargil War—opening a second front to facilitate the fighting in Kashmir, as occurred, for instance, during in 1965 during the second Indo-Pak war. As Sumit Ganguly noted:

> Through the Indian response was vigorous, it is important to note that the military were confronted with significant constraints of their actions… despite the availability of three strike corps, composed of sixty thousand soldiers broken down into three divisions each in the Punjab and Rajasthan, no orders were issued to open a second front.[92]

---

[89] Malik, *India's Military Conflicts and Diplomacy*, 252.

[90] Malik, *Kargil: From Surprise to Victory*, Chapter 11.

[91] Kapur, Ten Years of Instability in a Nuclear South Asia, 78.

[92] Ganguly & Kapur, *India, Pakistan, and the Bomb*, 48.

Eventually, the nuclear weaponization, i.e., the change in material power, was perceived differently by Islamabad and New Delhi. While Islamabad perceived the nuclear weaponization as a change in a relative power, which grants a shield against the conventionally superior enemy, New Delhi didn't perceive its own nuclear arsenal as an increase in its relative power. It perceived, however, the nuclear weaponization of its weaker enemy, Pakistan, as a constraint on its military conduct.

ISRAEL: A CASE OF NUCLEAR "IGNORANCE"

Pre-weaponization Period

Sinai War
On October 29, 1956, Israel launched the Sinai war (also known as Operation Kadesh), which lasted until November 7–6, when the cease-fire came into effect.[93] It was the most extensive Israeli military operation to date.[94] This operation was a result of a coordinated plan with France and Great Britain—two European powers, which strived to act against anticolonialist politics of the Egyptian President Nasser, which nationalized the Suez Canal.[95]

From the Israeli point of view, the cooperation with Paris and London was an opportunity to overcome its own security problems with Egypt. The biggest problem was the arms deal between Egypt and Czechoslovakia in 1955, which enabled Cairo to get advanced Soviet weapons.[96] Israeli decision-makers believed that after the absorption of new weapon systems, Egyptians would be able to attack Israel anytime they chose to do it. Under such circumstances, Israel didn't see any other option except preemptive first strike—attack on the Egyptian army prior to completion of absorption of the new weapons.[97]

---

[93] Moti Golani (1997). *There Will Be in the Summer War ... The Road to the Sinai War 1955–1956*, Tel Aviv: Maarahot, 438 [in Hebrew].

[94] Matti Greenberg (2006). The Background to the War, in Hagai Golan and Shaul Shay (Eds.), *50 Years Since the Sinai War*, Tel Aviv: Maarahot, 11 [in Hebrew].

[95] Maoz, *Defending the Holy Land*, 47.

[96] Aviezer Golan (2010). *Sinai Campaign*, Tel Aviv: Chief Education Officer, 6 [in Hebrew].

[97] Maoz, *Defending the Holy Land*, 51.

In addition to the Egyptian military buildup, Israel's security situation deteriorated during this period as well, due to the Fedayeen's activity, the Palestinian infiltration into the Israeli territory from Gaza strip and the West Bank for the purposes of terror and theft. This activity was supported and encouraged by the neighboring Arab states.[98] Although the infiltrators didn't come only from Egypt, many in Israeli politico-military establishment perceived this process to be sponsored primarily by Egypt, which used the frustration of Palestinians in Gaza as a fuel against Israel.[99] In this regard, the Sinai war against Egypt was an attempt to solve the infiltration problem.[100]

Finally, on the eve of the war Nasser closed the Straits of Tiran to Israeli shipping—the gateway for ships from Israeli southern port of Eilat to the Red Sea. This action was seen in Israel as an act of war.[101]

According to the operation plan coordinated with France and Great Britain, Israelis would advance into Sinai by parachuting a battalion near Mitla pass, about 30 kilometers east of Suez Canal. Afterwards, Great Britain and France would issue an ultimatum to both sides to withdraw their forces. The supposed Egypt's refusal would serve as an excuse for British–French intervention. Accordingly, British and French forces would land in the Suez Canal and bombard Egyptian Air Force.[102]

The Israeli operation, which began on October 29, surprised Egypt, which was expecting only a combined British–French attack, without Israeli involvement.[103] Israeli army quickly advanced to Sinai and Gaza.[104] Over the next few days, the Israelis advanced and conquered a number of targets in the depths of Sinai territory. On October 31, the Israeli defeated Egyptian force in Mitla pass.[105] On November 1 at

---

[98] Dayan, *Sinai Campaign Diary*, 12.

[99] Maoz, *Defending the Holy Land*, 49.

[100] Edward Luttwak & Dan Horowitz (1975). *The Israeli Army*, New York: Harper & Row Publishers, 140.

[101] Dayan, *Sinai Campaign Diary*, 17–18.

[102] Maoz, *Defending the Holy Land*, 47.

[103] Dayan, *Sinai Campaign Diary*, 40.

[104] Zaki Shalom (2006). The Forgotten War—Operation Kadesh and Its Political and Strategic Influences, in Hagai Golan & Shaul Shay (Eds.), *50 Years since the Sinai War*, Tel Aviv: Maarahot, 280 [in Hebrew].

[105] Kober, *Military Decision in Israeli-Arabs Wars 1948–1982*, 235.

night, Rafah town was occupied as well.[106] On November 3, the IDF completed the occupation of the Gaza Strip.[107] On the same day the air bombings of the British and French began.[108] On November 5 the Israeli army occupied Sharm el-Sheikh and completed the occupation of most of the Sinai Peninsula.[109] The occupation of Sharm el-Sheikh also meant the removal of the Egyptian blockade on the straits of Tiran—one of Israel's war aims.[110] In course of the war, Israel managed to occupy more territory than it had before. At the end of the military campaign, the Israeli army was located 15 kilometers east of the Suez Canal and along it.[111]

To summarize it up, during this war most of the characteristics of the Israeli warfighting pattern were reflected. The strategy of Israeli military was offensive in nature: Israel escalated the conflict and implemented first strike strategy. The war was transferred to the enemy territory, away from Israel's borders. Additionally, the Israelis strived to reach quick decision and thus to prevent protracted war.[112] As General Dayan, the Chief of Staff during the war, noted:

> Our goal is to bring down the enemy as quickly as possible and gain complete control of the Sinai Peninsula.[113]

The dimension of time was also an important component, derived from the Israeli concern of superpowers' intervention.[114]

Six-Day War

The next conventional war, the Six-Day War, occurred 11 years after Operation Kadesh and was a demonstration of Israel's military doctrine

---

[106] Kober, *Military Decision in Israeli-Arabs Wars 1948–1982*, 238.

[107] Dayan, *Sinai Campaign Diary*, 137.

[108] Dayan, *Sinai Campaign Diary*, 88.

[109] Kober, *Military Decision in Israeli-Arabs Wars 1948–1982*, 239.

[110] Dayan, *Sinai Campaign Diary*, 169.

[111] Golan, *Sinai Campaign*, 21.

[112] Kober, *Military Decision in Israeli-Arabs Wars 1948–1982*, 257; Golan, *Sinai Campaign*, 61.

[113] Dayan, *Sinai Campaign Diary*, 38.

[114] Golan, *Sinai Campaign*, 35.

effectiveness.[115] The outbreak of the war was preceded by a number of troubling events for Israel. Given the tensions on the Syrian–Israeli border, the Soviets warned Cairo and Damascus on May 12 or 13 1967, stating that Israel was concentrating forces on the border with Syria aiming to attack them supposedly between May 15 and May 22.[116] This Soviet move caused a chain reaction in the Middle East. On May 14, Egyptian military forces began to move forward toward Sinai. The Egyptian infantry and armor divisions crossed the Suez Canal. Moreover, Israelis received information on transferring Egyptian bombers to the Bir Tamada base in Sinai.[117] The deployment of the Egyptian units constituted a violation of Egyptian–Israeli tacit understandings after Israeli withdrawal from Sinai Peninsula following the war in 1956 regarding the demilitarization of Sinai Peninsula.[118]

The crisis worsened two days later, while Egypt required that the United Nations Forces, positioned as a buffer between Israel and Egypt following the end of the Sinai War, would evacuate its positions on the Israeli-Egypt border.[119] These developments contributed to the assessment in Israel, that this is not a defensive deployment of the Egyptian army, or reaction to events on the Syrian border, but rather preparations for the offensive operation.[120] Further escalation of the crisis occurred on 22 May upon Egypt's announcement of the blockade of the Tiran Straits—an Israeli official *casus bello*.[121]

Consequently, on June 4, 1967, the Israeli government ordered the army to perform the first strike.[122] The war began with a surprise attack on the Egyptian military airports by the Israeli Air Force on June 5, at 7:45 a.m.[123] In response to the Jordanian and Syrian attempts to bomb

[115] Michael Handel (July 1973). *Israel's Political-Military Doctrine*, Occasional Papers in International Affairs, 30, Cambridge: Harvard University—Center for International Affairs, 51.

[116] Shimon Golan (2007). *War on Three Fronts: Decision-Making in High Command During the Six Day War*, Tel Aviv: Maarahot, 53 [in Hebrew].

[117] Michael Oren (2004). *Six Days of War*, Or Yehuda: Dvir, 89 [Hebrew].

[118] Maoz, *Defending the Holy Land*, 80.

[119] Tal, *National Security*, 48.

[120] Golan (2007). *War on Three Fronts*, 68.

[121] Maoz, *Defending the Holy Land*, 80.

[122] Maoz, *Defending the Holy Land*, 81.

[123] Oren, *Six Days of War*, 212.

Israeli territory, Israel attacked their airports as well.[124] As a result of the Israeli airstrikes, the air forces of these three Arab states have ceased to exist as operational forces.

Afterward, the massive and rapid advancement of the Israeli ground forces deep into Sinai Peninsula has commenced on the ground. On June 5 in course of the invasion of Gaza, the Israeli forces captured Khan Yunis town in Gaza Strip.[125] Later that day, it was reported that the Israelis had entered Rafah.[126] Already on June 7, the third day of fighting, IDF forces captured Sharm el-Sheikh.[127] This has led to the removal of blockade of Tiran Straits.[128] In fact, 24 hours after Israel's air raids, the Egyptian defense in the Sinai Peninsula collapsed.[129] The rapid penetration of the Israelis into Sinai caused the Egyptian military command to order withdrawal of their forces.[130] At the end, the Israeli army occupied the Sinai Peninsula and the Gaza Strip.

The Israeli military achievements were even more remarkable if we compare Egypt's army collapse and the defeat of the Nazi African Corps of Rommel by the allies during the World War II. While the Egyptian army was 4 times bigger than Rommel's African Corps, Israelis defeated it in just 48 hours compared to six months needed for the defeat of the Germans in Africa.[131]

At the Jordanian front, the Israeli offensive effort has progressed even faster. In this respect, the Israeli army transferred the war to the enemy territory as well. On June 7, Nablus and East Jerusalem, including the Old City, were conquered.[132] At the same time, the Jordanians began to withdraw their troops from the West to the East Bank of the Jordan River. It should be noted, that already on the second day of fighting, in light of the Israeli achievements, the Jordanian command concluded that it had to withdraw the forces because otherwise they would

[124] Luttwak & Horowitz, *The Israeli Army*, 227.

[125] Luttwak & Horowitz, *The Israeli Army*, 271.

[126] Golan (2007). *War on Three Fronts*, 210.

[127] Oren, *Six Days of War*, 225.

[128] Oren, *Six Days of War*, 299.

[129] Kober, *Military Decision in Israeli-Arabs Wars 1948–1982*, 271.

[130] Luttwak & Horowitz, *The Israeli Army*, 227.

[131] Luttwak & Horowitz, *The Israeli Army*, 250.

[132] Luttwak & Horowitz, *The Israeli Army*, 259–270.

be destroyed. The Jordanian commander General Riyad urged King Hussein to urgently decide on the withdrawal:

> If we don't decide in twenty-four hours, you can say goodbye to your army and Jordan as a whole! We are on the verge of losing the West Bank; all our forces will be isolated and destroyed.[133]

On June 7, 1967, Israel gained control of Jerusalem and occupied territories in the West Bank.[134] After four days of fighting with the Jordanian army, the Israeli army managed to move forward to the Jordan River.[135]

After the Egyptian and Jordanian armies were defeated, Israel's army offensive effort moved to the northern Syrian front. Fighting on this front was already taking place against the backdrop of an international pressure on Israeli government to announce the cease-fire.[136] Offensive operations against Syrian units lasted less than 30 hours.[137] The Israeli operation began on June 9, in course of which the IDF conquered the Golan Heights and ended with the conquest of the Syrian city of Quneitra on June 10.

As we demonstrated, the conduct of the Israeli military matched its traditional pattern of conventional warfighting. The preference of offensive warfighting pattern was derived from the strategic culture perceptions of decision-makers in Israel. According to General Israel Tal, who participated in the war, the warfighting pattern reflected the basic Israeli assumptions about asymmetry: the lack of strategic depth and the need to transfer the war to the enemy's territory; striving to reach a decision as quickly as possible.[138] As Israeli Prime Minister, Levi Eshkol, emphasized at a cabinet meeting, held in the morning on June 4, 1967, a few hours before the outbreak of the war:

[133] Oren, *Six Days of War*, 273.

[134] Luttwak & Horowitz, *The Israeli Army*, 259–260.

[135] Oren, *Six Days of War*, 310.

[136] Oren, *Six Days of War*, 351.

[137] Luttwak & Horowitz, *The Israeli Army*, 272.

[138] Tal, *National Security*, 143.

We are no more than 2.5 million here, even if we take everything we have... even if the Arabs think of us as great heroes, that our guys can do anything ... [There is] a quantitative asymmetry of 1 to 3.[139]

Similarly the Defense Minister Moshe Dayan, at the time, noted:

There is nevertheless a limit to our ability to beat the Arabs. There is a limit not only to the human lives price, but there is a limit to the extent to which the war in this small country can be won, given such small distances, whereas within few hours the heart of the state can be reached.[140]

At this meeting, the Minister of Labor, Yigal Alon, also referred to Israel's complicated geostrategic situation and mentioned the threat of Jordanian forces, which were close to Israeli strategic objects at the country's central part.

Based on these approaches, Israeli decision-makers did not see a defensive pattern as feasible and stressed at their discussions the advantage of offensive warfighting pattern. According to the then head of the military's Intelligence Directorate General Aaron Yariv, there was a perception at the time, that only offensive warfighting could assist Israel:

The estimation was that the balance of power would be in our favor if we could initiate and surprise. This did not mean that if we failed to initiate and surprise the matter would end in a downfall, but there was a feeling that if we initiate and surprise - our success would be greater.[141]

This view was also shared by Dayan:

What is to be decided is the following: first, the first strike, I am in favor of the surprise of the first strike, because if we get them a hundred aircraft out of action, these 100 aircraft are worth more than any extra weapon... The first strike will determine who will have large losses... but what is much

---

[139] Transcript of the Cabinet Meeting as the Security Cabinet, 4 June 1967 (Morning), http://www.archives.gov.il/archives/#/Archive/0b0717068031be32/File/0b071 7068526a92b/Item/090717068526a984. Accessed 10 October 2019 [in Hebrew].

[140] Transcript of the Cabinet Meeting as the Security Cabinet, 4 June 1967 (Morning).

[141] Raphael Cohen Almagor (2013). The Six Day War—Interviews with Prof. Shimon Shamir and General (ret.) Aharon Yariv, *Social Issues in Israel*, 15, 181 [in Hebrew].

more important ... it is the main chance to win the war. And I would like to say in this regard, that our only chance to win the war is that we will initiate and conduct it according to our principles.[142]

Therefore, similarly to October 1956, Israel preferred to offensively act against Egyptian, Jordanian, and Syrian armies in accordance with its traditional pattern of conventional warfighting.

Post-weaponization Period

The Yom Kippur War

The next war, the Yom Kippur war, broke out about 5 years after Israel crossed the nuclear weaponization threshold. After President Nasser's death in September 1970, the new Egyptian leader Anwar Sadat saw Nasser's pan-Arabism orientation and cooperation with the Soviet Union as a failed policy. Sadat wanted to change Egypt's strategic situation, i.e., to return Sinai occupied by Israel, to reopen the Suez Canal and to restore Egyptian dignity after the defeat in summer 1967.[143] The Syrian leadership, an ally of Egypt, also strived to restore its lost pride during the Six-Day War and to reinstate the control over the Golan Heights captured by the Israeli army.[144]

Compared to the two previous wars, the Yom Kippur war began differently for Israel. The war began on October 6, 1973, at 14:00 p.m. with simultaneous combined attack by Egyptian and Syrian armies, which included air strikes and artillery shelling.[145] Then the second phase of Egyptian–Syrian offensive operation has commenced: crossing of the Suez Canal by the Egyptian forces and Syrian attack on Israeli forces at the Golan Heights. The operation was conducted by infantry,

---

[142]Transcript of the Security Cabinet Meeting, 4 June 1967 (Afternoon), http://www.archives.gov.il/archives/#/Archive/0b0717068031be32/File/0b0717068526a92b/Item/090717068526a984. Accessed 10 October 2019 [in Hebrew].

[143]Elbridge Colby, Avner Cohen, William McCants, et al. (April 2013). *The Israeli "Nuclear Alert" of 1973: Deterrence and Signaling in Crisis*, CNA Analysis & Solutions, 8.

[144]Elbridge Colby, Avner Cohen, William McCants, et al., *The Israeli "Nuclear Alert" of 1973*, 11.

[145]Tal, *National Security*, 173.

mechanized troops, and commandos.[146] The Egyptian offensive effort was primarily aimed against Bar-Lev Line—the chain of fortifications, which was built by Israel before the war on the eastern side of the Suez Canal. On the first night after the war began, Egypt's army managed to capture some Israeli outpost and a narrow strip at the eastern bank of the Canal.[147] The Syrians broke the Israeli defense lines in the southern part of Golan.[148] On October 7, Israeli army began to prepare a counterattack on both Syrian and Egyptian front.[149] The counterattack, that began on the next day, was only partially successful: while on the Syrian front, Israeli forces succeeded to move forward to the Southern Golan, at the southern front the counterattack failed and the Israeli armor suffered significant causalities.[150] The relative success in the north allowed the Israeli army to recapture on October 9 the territories that were lost at the beginning of the war causing heavy casualties to Syrians. Then, on the night of October 10–11 Prime Minister Golda Meir decided to move deeper into Syria, toward Damascus.[151] The goal of the Israeli advance was to take advantage of the counterattack success and transfer the war into the enemy's territory, from which the Israeli military could threaten the Syrian capital, Damascus.[152] Israel's offensive effort lasted until the 12th of the month and was largely halted due to the intervention of Iraqi expedition forces, who assisted the Syrians.[153] Despite certain progress, on October 13 Israelis moved their fighting effort from the north to the Egyptian front.[154] On October 14, the Egyptian forces tried to attack, but failed and suffered heavy losses.[155] Subsequently, on October 15–16, the Israeli forces began to cross the Suez Canal.[156] During several days,

---

[146] Elhanan Oren (2013). *History of the Yom Kippur War*, Tel Aviv: Ministry of Defense, 123, 128 [in Hebrew].

[147] Kober, *Military Decision in Israeli-Arabs Wars 1948–1982*, 334.

[148] Abraham Rabinovich (2003). *The Yom Kippur War*, New York: Schoken Books, 169.

[149] Shimon Golan (2013). *The War on Yom Kippur: Decision-Making in the Supreme Command During the Yom Kippur War*, Ben Shemen: Modan, 431 [in Hebrew].

[150] Golan, *The War on Yom Kippur*, 534–535.

[151] Kober, *Military Decision in Israeli-Arabs Wars 1948–1982*, 341.

[152] Oren, *History of the Yom Kippur War*, 269–270.

[153] Oren, *History of the Yom Kippur War*, 283–287.

[154] Oren, *History of the Yom Kippur War*, 292.

[155] Golan, *The War on Yom Kippur*, 900.

[156] Kober, *Military Decision in Israeli-Arabs Wars 1948–1982*, 345–346.

three IDF divisions were transferred to the West Bank, using the wedge between the two Egyptian armies. Eventually, the cease-fire was reached on October 24, 1973.[157] The war that started under unfavorable conditions for Israel, ended when an Israeli army was 101 km east of Cairo and 40 km south-west to Damascus.[158]

So far, we have briefly reviewed the course Yom Kippur war. We shall examine below the Israel's warfighting pattern during the war. In fact, as abovementioned, it was already evident in the first days of the war that the way the Israeli military fought was different from two previous wars, in 1956 and 1967. The Israeli army did not fight according to a traditional warfighting pattern: an initiation of a first strike and transfer of the war into the enemy's territory. Israelis first absorbed the attack of the Egyptian–Syrian coalition before moving on to counterattack to reach a decision. Moreover, in contrast to the two previous wars, Israel demonstrated restraint before the outbreak of the war, did not escalate and even tried to calm the tensions down.

Two days prior to the war commencement during a meeting led by the Defense Minister, the Assistant Chief of the Intelligence Division estimated that war was not expected[159] and the Head of the Intelligence Division also denied the possibility that the Arabs would attack.[160] Nevertheless, on October 6 few hours before the outbreak of the war, the Israeli decision-makers have eventually received the information, that Egypt and Syria are willing to attack.[161] If so, why did Israel not take an advantage of the time left, between receiving the information on the Arab intentions and the war outbreak, and didn't strike first, as it were in two previous wars? Why didn't Israel escalate the conflict first, but rather chose to demonstrate restraint? What were the reasons for this? Did the country's nuclear arsenal, which was obtained as a result of the secret nuclear weaponization in 1968, play any role in the decision-makers' considerations regarding a preferred way of the military's action? Did the nuclear weaponization contribute to the deviation from the traditional warfighting pattern of the Israeli army?

---

[157] Golan, *The War on Yom Kippur*, 1264.

[158] Maoz, *Defending the Holy Land*, 151.

[159] Oren, *History of the Yom Kippur War*, 92–93.

[160] Abraham Rabinovich (2003). *The Yom Kippur War*, New York: Schoken Books, 56.

[161] Ronen Bergman & Gil Meltzer (2003). *The Yom Kippur War—Moment of Truth*, Tel Aviv: Miskal, 41 [in Hebrew].

In fact, prior to the war outbreak, the political-security leadership of the State of Israel faced a difficult dilemma: whether to choose the traditional warfighting pattern of taking the initiative and striking first, while transferring the war to the enemy's territory, or not. During the meeting with Prime Minister Meir, held on October 6 at 8:05 a.m., only few hours before the outbreak of the war, Defense Minister Dayan expressed the dilemma regarding the first strike option:

> As for the preventive [first] strike, a preventative strike is of course a huge advantage. It will save many lives. If we go into a war and have first to defend ourselves - and I have confidence that we will stand up - and then attack, it will be a serious war.
>
> ... It is very tempting to me ... We have four hours to talk to the Americans. If they come to the same conclusions as us, if they [Arabs] attack tonight - that's their achievement. By noon, the Americans may say that the attack is certain and then we may be able to strike first.[162]

If the first strike would be a preferred option, why did Israel choose to first absorb the Arabs' attack? Based on the assumption regarding the nuclear weaponization impact, in the interstate conflict in the event of possession of nuclear weapons by one state only, a country which crossed a nuclear weaponization threshold and exclusively possesses nuclear arsenal will not necessarily perceive the acquired nuclear capability as a change of relative power *vis-à-vis* its stronger in conventional level enemies. Under such circumstances, such state will not see nuclear weapons as an alternative or a compensation to its conventional inferior capabilities. This situation demonstrates the *"Nuclear Ignorance"* model of the nuclear weaponization influence on the state's warfighting patterns: as long as the conflict remains at the conventional level, without a nuclear acquisition by an adversary, such country will tend to remain with the existing warfighting pattern.

Therefore, it is reasonable to assume that in the Israeli case, as a country that currently exclusively possess nuclear arsenal, the nuclear weaponization didn't in some way affect the preference of a warfighting pattern of the Israeli military. As elaborated in Chapter 3 above,

---

[162]Transcript of the Meeting with the Prime Minister, 6 October 1973 (8:05 a.m.), http://www.haaretz.co.il/hasite/images/yk%206%2010%2008%2005%20.pdf. Accessed 25 October 2019 [in Hebrew].

according to Generals Zeira and Shafir the nuclear arsenal could not have had any impact since it was never a factor in considerations of Israeli senior military command. Furthermore, in the recently published research, Avner Cohen and William Burr argued, that during Yom Kippur War in October 1973 the Israeli decision-makers realized that country's small nuclear arsenal wasn't suitable and relevant in course of the war.[163] Thus, as noted by Zeev Maoz, it is reasonable to assume, that only after the war and as part of the lessons learning process, Israeli strategic planners began to consider the tactical use of nuclear weapon at a battlefield and Israeli military planners started to regard the nuclear weapon as designed to prevent a major defeat in a conventional war.[164] Nevertheless, to date there is no evidence or support for the assumption, that nuclear weapons have been integrated into the Israeli military, as it is in the American and Russian armies. Moreover, Vipin Narang noted, that nuclear arsenal was not incorporated in the Israeli military and embedded in its doctrine. This decision was made by Ben-Gurion and later adopted by Prime Minister Eshkol.[165]

It should be noted, that despite the fact, that the nuclear weaponization didn't affect the warfighting pattern of the Israeli army, the Yom Kippur war is still associated with the nuclear context. It appears to be an episode, which allegedly occurred at the very first stages of the fighting. Upon the failure of a counterattack on the southern front, a pessimistic atmosphere prevailed among the Israeli command regarding the chances to prevail in the war. In this regard, in 1976 an article stating that in light of the failure of the counterattack, Israel deployed "Jericho" missiles with nuclear warheads, was published in the "Time" magazine.[166] Seymour Hersh in his book "*The Samson Option*" wrote:

---

[163]William Burr, Avner Cohen, Kar-Erik DE Geer (2019, September 22). Blast from the Past, *Foreign Policy*, https://foreignpolicy.com/2019/09/22/blast-from-the-past-vela-satellite-israel-nuclear-double-flash-1979-ptbt-south-atlantic-south-africa/. Accessed 29 September 2019.

[164]Maoz, *Defending the Holy Land*, 165.

[165]Vipin Narang (2014). *Nuclear Strategy in the Modern Area*, Princeton: Princeton University Press, 184.

[166]William Schwartz & Charles Derber (1993). *The Nuclear Seduction*, Berkley and Los Angeles: University of California Press, 109.

The Israeli leadership, faced with its greatest crisis in the history of the country, has instructed to arm and target its nuclear arsenal in the event of total collapse and subsequent need for the Samson Option.[167]

A study published in 2013 by a group of researchers, headed by Avner Cohen, found, however, no confirmation of Hersh's claims, including his claim that the Israeli ambassador in Washington, Simcha Dinitz, "blackmailed" the US administration in a threat to escalate the conflict with the Arabs to a nuclear level. This assessment is based primarily on the statement of William Quandt, who was a member of the US National Security Council during the Yom Kippur war. As he recalls:

I was close enough to those events as a member of the National Security Council staff that I doubt that an explicit threat was made by [Israeli Ambassador Simcha] Dinitz [as alleged by Hersh]. We did know around this time, however, that Israel had placed its Jericho missiles on alert. I did not know what kind of warheads they had, but it did not make much sense to me that they would be equipped with conventional ordnance. I assume others agreed. It was also conceivable that a nuclear threat might be made if Egyptian troops broke through at the passes [that is, deeper in the Sinai and thus closer to Israel proper]. None of this had to be spelled out in so many words by the Israelis.

It is true that for one day, October 9, there was a sense of panic among some Israeli leaders.[168]

The research also concluded the following:

...it is plausible, and in our assessment likely that the Israelis modified the status of their nuclear delivery systems, especially their Jericho ballistic missile force, in a manner consistent with the overall changes to their military posture in response to the Arab assaults. In other words, the Israelis probably prepared or checked their nuclear delivery systems in response to the Arab attacks in order to prepare them for any eventuality, a sensible precautionary move during a large-scale attack.[169]

---

[167] Hersh, *The Samson Option*, 166.

[168] Elbridge Colby, Avner Cohen, William McCants, et al., *The Israeli "Nuclear Alert" of 1973*, 34.

[169] Elbridge Colby, Avner Cohen, William McCants, et al., *The Israeli "Nuclear Alert" of 1973*, 34.

Azaryahu Arnan (Sinai), Assistant Minister Israel Galili, who was a member of the security cabinet during the war and Prime Minister Golda Meir's closest political ally, recalled in an interview with Avner Cohen, that at the end of the cabinet meeting on October 7 was discussed a probability to demonstrate the Israeli nuclear capability:

> "Sini recalled that he was waiting outside the Prime Minister's office in Tel Aviv late in the morning or early in the afternoon of October 7 for his boss, Minister Galili, who was attending a war cabinet meeting (or informal consultation) inside as the situation on the Golan reached its nadir for Israel… After the war cabinet meeting adjourned, Galili shared with Sini the unusual events that had taken place inside as the meeting finished… As the discussion appeared to reach closure and some of the senior military officers and senior civil servants started to leave the room (apparently including Chief of Staff David Elazar), Defense Minister Dayan asked Prime Minister Meir if she would permit him to bring in Israeli Atomic Energy Commission Director-General Shalhevet Freier to "brainstorm" with her and the three ministers in the war cabinet (Minister of Defense Dayan, Deputy Prime Minister Yigal Alon, and the Minister without portfolio Israel Galili) about possible "demonstration options," an apparent reference to a demonstration of Israel's nuclear weapons capability."[170]

According to Arnan, in response to Dayan's recommendation, Meir refused to discuss these options.

Due to the taboo surrounding the nuclear issue in Israel, it is not possible to accurately assess whether there was a change in the country's nuclear preparedness and if so, what was its nature. In any case, the Israeli army has ignored its nuclear capability when it comes to conventional warfighting. In other words, the nuclear weaponization neither encouraged aggression nor imposed restraints. Israeli still considered to strike first, as previously. If so, the question remains what caused the change in warfighting pattern?

Prime Minister Golda Meir, who also considered the feasibility of first strike strategy at the abovementioned meeting shortly before the war, noted:

> A preventive strike – is very attractive. But it is not 1967. This time the world is revealed in all its despair. They won't believe us.

[170]Elbridge Colby, Avner Cohen, William McCants, et al., *The Israeli "Nuclear Alert" of 1973*, 42–43.

According to Meir, the fear of losing international support, especially of the United States, contributed to a change in preference of the war-fighting pattern. Israel was afraid that if it started the war it would be accused of escalation and lose American support. In retrospect, after the war, Moshe Dayan expressed the same fear of losing American support as a result of a first strike:

> I was concerned that these actions, a hit and a full mobilization could jeopardize our chances of receiving full US support.[171]

Deputy Chief of Staff General during the war Israel Tal also similarly noted:

> We can't be the first ones to fire if I think what Americans will say.[172]

These statements by the Israeli senior politicians and officers indicate, that prior to the outbreak of war, the first strike option was considered. The logic behind this option was the same as the decision-makers' considerations before the outbreak of the Sinai war and the Six-Day War and derived from strategic culture perceptions regarding the strategic threat—in view of the asymmetry *vis-à-vis* Arab military forces to improve Israel's chance to reach decision of the enemies by taking the initiative. It is clear that the considerations of the superpower's support (and not the nuclear dimension) caused to the adoption of the restraint and the defensive warfighting pattern.

REFERENCES

Abid Ali, Lubnan. (July–December 2009). The Rann of Kutch and Its Aftermath. *A Research Journal of South Asian Studies*, 24/2, 2250–25652.

Adnan, Mubeen. (2015). The Kargil Crisis and Pakistan's Constraints. *Journal of Political Studies*, 22/1, 129–151.

Amin, A. H. (1999). *The 1947–48 Kashmir War: The War of Lost Opportunities*. Lahore: Strategicus and Tacticus. https://archive.org/stream/The1947-48KashmirWarTheWarOfLostOpportunities/49202996-The-1947-48-Kashmir-War-Revised_djvu.txt. Accessed 26 October 2019.

[171] Oren, *History of the Yom Kippur War*, 103.

[172] Golan, *The War on Yom Kippur*, 67.

Bergman, R. & Meltzer, G. (2003). *The Yom Kippur War—Moment of Truth*. Tel Aviv: Miskal [in Hebrew].

Bose, S. (2003). *Kashmir: Roots of Conflict, Paths to Peace*. Cambridge and London: Harvard University Press.

Brines, R. (1968). *The Indo-Pakistani Conflict*. London: Pall Mall Press.

Burr, W., Cohen, A., & De Geer, K. (2019, September 22). Blast from the Past. *Foreign Policy*. https://foreignpolicy.com/2019/09/22/blast-from-the-past-vela-satellite-israel-nuclear-double-flash-1979-ptbt-south-atlantic-south-africa/. Accessed 29 September 2019.

Cohen Almagor, R. (2013). The Six Day War—Interviews with Prof. Shimon Shamir and General (ret.) Aharon Yariv. *Social Issues in Israel*, 15, 171–195 [in Hebrew].

Colby, E., Cohen, A., McCants, W., et al. (April 2013). *The Israeli "Nuclear Alert" of 1973: Deterrence and Signaling in Crisis*. CNA Analysis & Solutions.

Dayan, M. (1967). *Sinai Campaign Diary*. Tel Aviv: Am Hasefer [in Hebrew].

Fair, Christine. (2019). Militants in the Kargil Conflict: Myths, Realities, and Impacts. In Peter Lavoy (Ed.), *Asymmetric Warfare in South Asia* (pp. 231–257). Cambridge University Press.

Ganguli, S. (1986). *The Origins of War in South Asia: Indo-Pakistani Conflicts Since 1947*. Boulder and London: Westview Press.

Ganguli, S. & Hagerty, D. (2005). *Fearful Symmetry: India-Pakistan Crises in the Shadow of Nuclear Weapons*. Seattle: University of Washington Press.

Ganguly, S. & Kapur, P. (2010). *India, Pakistan, and the Bomb*. New York: Columbia University Press.

Gauhar, A. (1996). *Ayub Khan: Pakistan's First Military Ruler*. Karahi: Oxford University Press.

Golan, A. (2010). *Sinai Campaign*. Tel Aviv: Chief Education Officer [in Hebrew].

Golan, S. (2007). *War on Three Fronts: Decision-Making in High Command During the Six Day War*. Tel Aviv: Maarahot [in Hebrew].

Golan, S. (2013). *The War on Yom Kippur: Decision-Making in the Supreme Command During the Yom Kippur War*. Ben Shemen: Modan [in Hebrew].

Golani, M. (1997). *There Will Be in the Summer War … The Road to the Sinai War 1955–1956*. Tel Aviv: Maarahot [in Hebrew].

Greenberg, M. (2006). The Background to the War. In Hagai Golan & Shaul Shay (Eds.), *50 Years Since the Sinai War* (pp. 11–14). Tel Aviv: Maarahot [in Hebrew].

Handel, M. (July 1973). *Israel's Political-Military Doctrine*. Occasional Papers in International Affairs, 30. Cambridge: Harvard University—Center for International Affairs.

Hersh, S. (1991). *The Samson Option: Israel's Nuclear Arsenal and American Foreign Policy*. Tel Aviv: Yedioth Ahronoth.

Jones, S. & Fair, C. (2010). *Counterinsurgency in Pakistan*. Santa Monica: Rand.

Oren, M. (2004). *Six Days of War*. Or Yehuda: Dvir [in Hebrew].

Kapur, P. (Fall 2008). Ten Years of Instability in a Nuclear South Asia. *International Security*, 33/2, 71–94.

Kapur, P. & Ganguly, S. (Summer 2012). The Jihad Paradox: Pakistan and Islamist Militancy in South Asia. *International Security*, 37/1, 114–141.

Kasturi, B. (2008). The State of War with Pakistan. In Daniel Martson & Chandar Sundaram (Eds.), *A Military History of India and South Asia* (pp. 139–156). Bloomington and Indianapolis: Indiana University Press.

Khan, F. H. (Spring 2003). Challenges to Nuclear Stability in South Asia. *The Nonproliferation Review*, 59–74.

Khan, F. H. (2012). *Eating Grass. The Making of the Pakistani Bomb*. Stanford: Stanford California Press.

Lamb, A. (1991). *Kashmir: A Disputed Legacy*. Hertfordshire: Roxford Books.

Ludwig. W. (2015). Indian Military Modernization and Conventional Deterrence in South Asia. *The Journal of Strategic Studies*, 38/5, 729–772.

Luttwak, E. & Horowitz, D. (1975). *The Israeli Army*. New York: Harper & Row Publishers.

Malik, General V. P. (2006). *Kargil: From Surprise to Victory*. New Delhi: HarperCollins Publishers India.

Malik, General V. P. (2016). *India's Military Conflicts and Diplomacy*. New Delhi: HarperCollins Publishers India.

Maoz, Z. (2009). *Defending the Holy Land*. Ann Arbor: The University of Michigan Press.

Mir, M. A. (April 2014). India-Pakistan: The History of Unsolved Conflicts. *IOSR, Journal of Humanities and Social Science*, 19/4, 101–110.

Narang, V. (2014). *Nuclear Strategy in the Modern Area*. Princeton: Princeton University Press.

Nawaz, S. (2008). *Crossed Swords: Pakistan, Its Army, and the Wars Within*. Oxford: Oxford University Press.

Oren, E. (2013). *History of the Yom Kippur War*. Tel Aviv: Ministry of Defense [in Hebrew].

Rabinovich, A. (2003). *The Yom Kippur War*. New York: Schoken Books.

Schwartz, W. & Derber, C. (1993). *The Nuclear Seduction*. Berkley and Los Angeles: University of California Press.

Shalom, Z. (2006). The Forgotten War—Operation Kadesh and Its Political and Strategic Influences. In Hagai Golan & Shaul Shay (Eds.), *50 Years Since the Sinai War* (pp. 279–305). Tel Aviv: Maarahot [in Hebrew].

Singh, L. (1979). *Indian Sword Strikes in East Pakistan*. Ghaziabad: Vikas Publishing.

Singh, R. (Autumn 2012). Operations in Jammu and Kashmir 1947–48. *Scholar Warrior*, 130–158.

Subramaniam, A. (2016). *India's Wars: A Military History 1947–1971.* Noida: HarperCollins Publishers India.

Tal, I. (1996). *National Security: Few vs. Many.* Tel Aviv: Dvir.

Tasleem, S. (2016, June 30). Pakistan's Nuclear Use Doctrine. https://carnegieendowment.org/2016/06/30/pakistan-s-nuclear-use-doctrine-pub-63913. Accessed 12 November 2019.

"Pakistan Was to Deploy Nukes Against India During Kargil War". (2018, July 12). https://economictimes.indiatimes.com/news/defence/pakistan-was-to-deploy-nukes-against-india-during-kargil-war/articleshow/50019153.cms?-from=mdr. Accessed 12 November 2019.

Report on Nuclear Safety, Nuclear Stability and Nuclear Strategy in Pakistan. (2002, January 14). https://pugwash.org/2002/01/14/report-on-nuclear-safety-nuclear-stability-and-nuclear-strategy-in-pakistan/. Accessed 12 November 2019.

Transcript of the Cabinet Meeting as the Security Cabinet, 4 June 1967 (Morning). http://www.archives.gov.il/archives/#/Archive/0b0717068031be32/File/0b0717068526a92b/Item/090717068526a984. Accessed 10 October 2019 [in Hebrew].

Transcript of the Cabinet Meeting as the Security Cabinet, 4 June 1967 (Afternoon). http://www.archives.gov.il/archives/#/Archive/0b0717068031be32/File/0b0717068526a92b/Item/090717068526a984. Accessed 10 October 2019 [in Hebrew].

Transcript of the Meeting with the Prime Minister, 6 October 1973 (8:05 a.m.). http://www.haaretz.co.il/hasite/images/yk%206%2010%2008%2005%20.pdf. Accessed 25 October 2019 [in Hebrew].

CHAPTER 7

Summary and Conclusions

Abstract This chapter is a concluding discussion of the main findings. The chapter refers to the book's contribution to scholarly literature on nuclear weapons, which suffered for years from a so-called "Cold War hangover" focusing to a large extent on the experience of two super-powers—the United States and the USSR. Subsequently, we discuss the theoretical framework implemented in the study involving external and internal variables. The discussion then focuses on a comparative examination of the material power of the examined case studies. We proceed with the examination of the countries' perceptions of their relative power. Then we summarize the nuclear weaponization influence through the brief review of the patterns of warfighting of Pakistan, India, and Israel before and after crossing the nuclear weapons threshold.

Keywords NATO · Nuclear weaponization influence · Patterns of warfighting · Relative power perception · Second nuclear proliferation wave

This book introduced a model for understanding the influence of a nuclear weaponization on the patterns of warfighting in course of conventional conflicts. For the purposes of the study, we focused on three case studies—Pakistan, India, and Israel. These are three countries, which belong to the second nuclear proliferation wave, crossed

© The Author(s) 2020   151
I. Davidzon, *Patterns of Conventional*
Warfighting under the Nuclear Umbrella,
https://doi.org/10.1007/978-3-030-45594-1_7

secretly the nuclear weaponization threshold even prior to the public demonstration of their nuclear capability via the performance of public nuclear tests. Therefore, for these countries, which belong to the second nuclear proliferation wave, a secret nuclear weaponization was a highly important and influential milestone in their nuclear development. In the case studies of India and Pakistan, it took several years for these two countries to publicly demonstrate their nuclear capabilities. As for Israel, no public test has been conducted and this country didn't officially acknowledge the existence of its own nuclear arsenal. Nevertheless, refraining from conducting a public nuclear test does not derogate from the fact that Pakistan, India, and Israel are nuclear-armed states. Due to the technological development, a state can acquire nuclear capability without the necessity to conduct a public test.

In view of such exceptional conduct, we did not regard the experience of the first wave proliferation states as a point of reference for analyzing the military conduct of the three examined countries before and after crossing the nuclear weaponization threshold. Those countries introduce a different mode of a nuclear weapon acquisition compared to the second wave countries model of a nuclear weapon acquisition—they obtained nuclear arsenal in course of the public tests and no clandestine process of nuclear weaponization preceded this. Moreover, although there is plenty of literature on the NPT's five nuclear weapons states, its focus on the effect of nuclear weapon on deterrence with the emphasis on a nuclear war prevention, seems to be irrelevant for examining the warfighting patterns during conventional conflicts under the nuclear umbrella. In this sense, this book can be seen as a further contribution to scholarly literature on nuclear weapons, which suffered from a so-called "Cold War hangover," dealing largely with the experience of two superpowers—the United States and the USSR.[1]

Furthermore, the decision to implement the research model based on causal mechanism involving external and internal variables was motivated by a few factors. First, the existing theories, mainly optimistic and pessimistic approaches regarding nuclear weapon proliferation seem not to be applicable for the purposes of examination of a nuclear weaponization influence on the countries' warfighting patterns. Both approaches do not extend the discussion beyond the influence of the nuclear

---

[1] Narang, *Nuclear Strategy in the Modern Era*, 2.

weapons on deterrence, conflict stability, and probability of war. While focusing mainly on the question whether nuclear proliferation increases or decreases a probability of wars among nuclear states, the optimists/ pessimists debate paid less attention to the question how nuclear weaponization affects the countries' conventional warfighting and less stressed the issue of variability of countries warfighting patterns under the nuclear umbrella.

Similarly, the approach of the stability–instability paradox is also inapplicable for examining the influence of nuclear weaponization on warfighting patterns of the Pakistani, Indian, and Israeli militaries. Its logic that lower nuclear stability decreases the possibility of conventional conflicts and vice versa, is inconsistent, among others, with the Indo-Pakistani reality as well. Such logic would undermine the essence of Pakistan's view of the role of the nuclear weapons. Islamabad adopted the first use nuclear weapons policy to deter conventionally stronger India. This means that lower probability of nuclear war, i.e., nuclear stability, would reduce the credibility of Pakistan's deterrence. Additionally, the stability–instability paradox cannot explain the aggressive, offensive pattern of warfighting, which the Pakistani army continued to implement in the post-weaponization period as well.

Furthermore, similarly to the optimistic and pessimistic approaches, the approach of stability–instability paradox referred to the situation, in which two or more advisories possess a military nuclear capability. It ignores, however, the situation in which only one side in the conflict possesses a nuclear weapon. Thus, such approach seems to be inapplicable to the Middle East region, where only Israel holds a nuclear arsenal.

To overcome these problems, we implemented the theoretical model based on the combination of the concept of a pre-existing strategic threat, consisting of material power components and a concept of strategic culture. For the purpose of the study, we made a distinction between mutual (Indo-Pakistani conflict) and exclusive (Israel-Arab conflict) nuclear weapon possession.

As noted, we used the definition of strategic culture based on the concept elaborated by Alastair Johnston. This definition provides the chain of causation between a cultural variable and a military behavior. Accordingly, a country's strategic culture is made up of two levels:

- Symbolic level—a set of beliefs and assumptions regarding geostrategic environment, country's self-image and the threat posed by an enemy.
- Operational level, which refers to assumptions regarding the efficiency of strategic options, the available patterns of warfighting.

The symbolic level of beliefs and assumptions is an informational basis for decision-makers to shape a perception of relative power *vis-à-vis* other adversaries. Pursuant to the symbolic level assumption, they chose from the variety of available warfighting patterns the preferred one.

According to my approach, the influence of the nuclear weaponization on the countries' warfighting patterns is discernible through three models:

- *Restraint Imposition* on a country, to proceed with its traditional pattern of warfighting against an aggressive nuclear-armed adversary.
- *Aggression Encouragement* of a weaker aggressive and revisionist country, which due to nuclear weaponization manages to maintain its traditional pattern of war management against a much stronger enemy.
- *Nuclear "Ignorance"*—a country adopts a warfighting pattern without reference to its military nuclear arsenal.

The nuclear weaponization influence takes place through the following causal mechanism. A nuclear weaponization constitutes a clear change in the pre-existing strategic threat, in countries' relative material power comprising of a geostrategic situation, size of armed forces and military budgets. It affects the warfighting patterns of the three examined armies, however, not directly but through variable perceptions of the decision-makers in Pakistan, India, and Israel. Based on their strategic culture perceptions (regarding geostrategic environment, a country's self-image and a threat posed by an enemy) they perceive the nuclear weaponization according to one of the abovementioned models of influence.

The analysis of the material strength of Pakistan shows a certain similarity to the Israeli case. Like Israel *vis-à-vis* the Arab states, Pakistan since its independence in 1947, has had significant asymmetry in terms of relative power *vis-à-vis* its prime enemy, India. Although Pakistan's territory is larger than Israel's, the common characteristic of the two countries in terms of the strategic geostrategic situation is the lack of a strategic depth. Due to such a problematic geostrategic situation, both countries were required to deal with the danger of a surprise attack, without their armies being sufficiently prepared on time.

It should be noted that since the execution of peace treaties with Israel's neighbors, Egypt and Jordan, due to the de facto dismantling of the Syrian army as a result of the civil war in the country and the US military's invasion of Iraq in 2003, Israel's strategic situation has improved. Nevertheless, during the 1950s, 1960s, and 1970s Israel had to face the threat of a combined Arab offensive. Given the size of its army and the military budget, Israel suffered from a quantitative asymmetry in armed forces and economic resources *vis-à-vis* the Arab countries. This trend has not changed over the years and even today, due to the security challenges, Israel invests a considerable portion of its budget for military purposes. The significant economic investment in military is mainly derived from Israel's desire to address the quantitative advantage of Arab states through a quality advantage.

With respect to Pakistan, while the size of its armed forces and military budget has been rising steadily over the decades, this does not affect the asymmetry between it and India. Therefore, given such asymmetry both Israel and Pakistan have an inferiority in all parameters of relative material power *vis-à-vis* their adversaries.

At the same time, asymmetry was perceived differently by the Pakistani and Israeli decision-makers and eventually led to different conclusions regarding a preferred pattern of conventional warfare.

Based on the concept of the two-nation theory of Muhammad Ali Jinnah, which excluded the possibility of coexistence of Muslim and Hindu communities within one state, Pakistanis saw no other option than the establishment of independent Pakistan, as an optimal solution for Muslims of the Indian subcontinent. The politico-military conflict with India was perceived within Pakistan's strategic culture as a continuation of the struggle with Hindus in the pre-independence period. The further image of India as an enemy and the perceptions of the country's geostrategic situation through the Indian threat are derived from beliefs and attitudes regarding the role of the Muslim state and the dispute over Kashmir area.

Based on such beliefs, Pakistani decision-makers perceive India's takeover of Kashmir as injustice, which contradicts the very idea behind the establishment of Pakistan. India's opposition regarding the freedom of self-determination of the Muslims in Kashmir is perceived as an attempt to undermine the very idea of the country as a Muslim national home. The image of India as an enemy is also reflected in the attitude in the Pakistani strategic culture regarding the country's geostrategic situation—there is a concern in the Pakistani strategic culture regarding the lack of strategic depth, the small and narrow territory of the country, and not less important the proximity of cities, lines of communication, and infrastructure to the border with hostile India.

Concerning Israel, the inferiority in the parameters of relative power resulted in the "siege mentality." The Israeli decision-makers adopted a self-image of "few versus many," which means a severe and incorrigible quantitative asymmetry between Israel and the Arab states. Subsequently, the dominant perception of the Arab enemies in the Israeli strategic culture is one of total and uncompromising hostility toward the Jewish country.

Moreover, despite the technological and political changes that occurred over the years, Israeli strategic culture attitudes and approaches remained unchanged. Although in recent years, in light of its nuclear ambitions and support for terrorist organizations in the Middle East, the Islamic Republic of Iran is also perceived in Israel through the prism of an enemy, the image of Arab states as an enemy remains constant. Thus, for instance the Prime Minister of Israel, Benjamin Netanyahu referring to the peace treaties with Jordan and Egypt stated that, "we have the same peace with Egypt and Jordan as a result of deterrence." According to this view, the Arab hostility toward Israel has not passed and cold peace with those states only exists because of Israel's military power.[2]

In light of the Israeli–Arab conflict, the geostrategic situation is perceived as problematic in terms of defense capability. The lack of strategic depth and small territory created a danger of invasion and occupation without prior warning. The problem of the lack of strategic depth is also relevant in the age of missiles.

Since the declaration of independence in August 1947 by Pakistan and India, both countries have continuously remained in mutually hostile relations.[3] Israel, since its independence proclamation in May 1948, was

[2] Tal Shilo (2019, November 11). Netanyahu on the Peace with Jordan: "It Is Important to Prevent the Takeover of Islamist Elements", *Walla News*, https://news.walla.co.il/item/3322959. Accessed 9 December 2019 [in Hebrew].

[3] Khan (Spring 2003). Challenges to Nuclear Stability in South Asia, 60.

forced as well to struggle for its existence. As noted, such complicated politico-military reality, mainly the pre-existing geostrategic threats, were perceived through the lens of the "siege mentality" and the two-nation theory, which are integrated into the Israeli and Pakistani strategic cultures, respectively. The decision-makers in Islamabad and Tel Aviv drew, however, different conclusions regarding their inferiority *vis-à-vis* their enemies and favored patterns of warfighting, which are consistent with their strategic cultures' beliefs and attitudes. While Israel has fought and even initiated wars to defend itself and maintain a status quo, Pakistan has initiated wars for the status quo change. Nevertheless, despite such varying perception of the strategic threat both countries adopted quite a similar pattern of warfighting patterns: despite some nuances, the Pakistani and Israeli armies adopted an offensive, with the tendency to escalation pattern of warfighting. Given the perception of quantitative inferiority in terms of relative power, both militaries preferred to initiate a conflict (either through Israel's fist strike strategy or the Pakistani use of irregular armed forces) as strategy to gain a relative advantage over a stronger foe.

As for India, its geostrategic situation is different from that of Israel and Pakistan. It has a large territory and doesn't have problems such as a lack of strategic depth. Its line of communications and military infrastructure are not situated in proximity to border with hostile countries, as in the Israeli and Pakistani cases. Despite these favorable conditions, however, the Indian geostrategic situation is influenced by the conflict with Pakistan. Thus, due to the fact that until 1971 Pakistan consisted of two separate parts, divided by the Indian territory, New Delhi had to consider the danger of war on two fronts simultaneously. After the third Indo-Pak War in 1971, this threat was removed.

India has also an advantage over Pakistan in the size of its armed forces. Despite some declines and increases, this asymmetry is maintained for decades over an average of 1–2 in favor of India. In the economic context, India has evolved from a poor country to one of the world's important economies. Its stronger economy allowed it to grant more resources to the armed forces, thus providing additional advantage over Pakistan, which is economically dependent on the international and the Saudi Arabian financial assistance.[4]

---

[4]Pakistan Should Protect Its National Interest Over Middle East Crisis (2020, January 7). *DAWN*, https://www.dawn.com/news/1526716/pakistan-should-protect-its-national-interest-over-middle-east-crisis. Accessed 8 January 2020.

In light of the above, the Indian strategic culture embeds a self-image of the country's greatness, both physical and civilizational. This image has been developed to the desire to be one of the strongest countries in the international arena. Such a desire does not mean that India adopted the policy of expansionism. On the contrary, despite the aspiration for a global status, India supports a policy of status quo. This policy doesn't exclude, however, the possibility of implementation of force. India's strategic culture admits that power and even violence constitute an integral part of relations among nations. Therefore, the important part of Indian strategic culture is an aggressive and assertive position toward any external attempt to undermine its territorial integrity or harm its interests.

Following the confrontation with the neighboring country, Pakistan, mainly due to the conflict over Kashmir, the image of the Muslim country as an enemy takes a central place in the strategic culture of New Delhi. This hostility toward Pakistan undoubtedly influenced the Indian decision-makers' attitude to the geostrategic situation, which was perceived by them through the lens of this hostility perception.

As a result of these cultural perceptions, India adopted a defensive, restrained pattern of warfighting with the tendency to escalation in the course of a conflict. It tended not to initiate armed conflicts but to respond to the aggression from outside, primly from Pakistan, on the one hand and to escalate in course of a conflict in order to defend national interest and sovereignty, on the other hand.

It should be noted that according, for instance, to the approach of offensive realism presented by Mearsheimer, it is less likely that the weaker party will attack the stronger party.[5] This means that it would be expected that a stronger state would act offensively. Thus, given the power gap between India and Pakistan, it was conceivable that the stronger country India would prefer an aggressive pattern of warfighting. In the case of Pakistan and Israel, it could be assumed that given the asymmetry, they would adopt a defensive and restrained warfighting pattern. By setting a direct causal link between a country's relative power and its military behavior, however, the offensive realism approach ignored the important variable of decision-makers' perception of relative power, which could "distort" such objective causal link. Furthermore, expanding a research beyond the material variables to the internal

[5] Mearsheimer, *The Tragedy of Great Power Politics*, 26.

strategic culture variable allows one to understand the reasons for a preference of a particular pattern of warfighting by the three countries. Due to their strategic culture perceptions both armies of Pakistan and Israel didn't choose defensive warfighting patterns, as it's predicted by the offensive realism but preferred to fight in line with the warfighting patterns, which characterized by offensive and escalation. Conversely, India adopted an offensive and restrained pattern of warfighting. These patters were recognizable during the wars fought by three armies in the pre-weaponization period of their history.

Consequently, the watershed of a nuclear weaponization affected differently each of the three examined countries. Due to the different strategic culture beliefs and attitudes, the change in the relative power associated with the nuclear weaponization was interpreted differently in Pakistan, India, and Israel. In contrast to the abovementioned existing theories and approaches that assume kind of deterministic effect of the nuclear weaponization impact on the states' military behavior—either caution encouragement or the logic of stability–instability paradox—the theoretical framework applied in this book has allowed to explain the variety in the impact of nuclear weaponization on patterns of conventional warfighting.

Pakistan perceived the nuclear weaponization as a kind of shield against the superior capabilities of the Indian military. Such perception allowed Pakistan's military to fight as previously, according to its pre-weaponization era warfighting pattern that matches the prevailed strategic culture attitudes. Nuclear weapons were interpreted by decision-makers in Islamabad as a factor that grants the Pakistani army the ability to take action against India's stronger army. Therefore, the nuclear weapon encouraged the Pakistani army to act aggressively according to the *Aggression Encouragement* model of nuclear weaponization influence. The nuclear weapon allowed a weaker state to persist with the existing pattern of offensive and escalating warfighting against the superior enemy, India. This was evident during the Kargil War in 1999. This does not necessarily mean that any country under conditions more or less similar to those of Pakistan would choose the same pattern of action. During the Cold War, in view of the Soviet Army's quantitative advantage, NATO adopted a similar approach of potentially using nuclear weapons in the event of a Soviet attack in Europe. But the difference is that in the Pakistani case this strategy was adopted to challenge the status quo and not to preserve it. The reason for this difference lies in Pakistan's strategic culture, with its emphasis on Kashmir and the perception of India as an enemy.

In contrast to the case of the Pakistani army, the Indian army's conduct in the war was quite different. The nuclear weaponization affect caused the "Weak-Strong Actors Paradox." The superior military capabilities of New Delhi were offset by the nuclear weapon of the weaker one. This reflects the *Restraint Imposition* model of nuclear weaponization. As aforementioned, during Kargil war the Indian army was restrained from escalating the conflict, it was requested by the government to refrain from geographically expanding the conflict and crossing the international border. Such deviation occurred due to the change in perception of relative power—India faced now a nuclear-armed aggressive and revisionist enemy. Given this new reality, the Indian army changed its preference of warfighting pattern and demonstrated in 1999 during Kargil War an updated one under the strategic culture stipulations. India did not initiate the war, but rather only responded to the Pakistani invasion—which corresponds to the first characteristic of the Indian warfighting pattern. On the other hand, it refrained from geographic expanding the conflict. In line with the assumptions of its strategic culture, New Delhi has responded to the violation of its sovereignty by Pakistani forces, however, given the entry of nuclear weapons into the conflict it hasn't escalated the conflict as it did in past and demonstrated restraint. In other words, the introduction of a nuclear weapon into conflict dynamic by Pakistan has resulted in a change in preference of warfighting pattern: under the strategic culture assumptions, the Indian army adjusted military conduct to the reality of nuclear umbrella deployed over the subcontinent.

In contrary to the Pakistani and Indian case studies, in the Israeli case nuclear weaponization seems not to have an effect on the country's military warfighting patterns. This situation reflects the features of "*Nuclear Ignorance*" model of nuclear weaponization on the conventional warfighting pattern. The nuclear weaponization hasn't caused a change in Israeli decision-makers' perception of its relative power. Moreover, possession of nuclear weapons did not become a factor in the decision-making process at the military level. Although it would be expected that Israel as a weaker state in terms of relative power in its conflict with the Arab countries will perceive a nuclear weapon as a shield against the superior capabilities of its enemies (as in the case with Pakistan), the Israeli army didn't refer to this ultimate weapon in its military planning and the nuclear capability was ignored. The nuclear weapon wasn't perceived by the Israeli decision-makers as compensating for its weakness. Indeed, in Yom Kippur War in October 1973, the Israeli army deviated from its traditional warfighting pattern—it didn't escalate and initiate the war. Nevertheless, the army chose to absorb the combined Egyptian–Syrian offensive not because of the nuclear weaponization, which occurred several years before the war, but due to the concern about the US support of Israel.

In view of the unchanged relative power perception of the Israeli decision-makers, the Israeli case study also contradicts with a direct causal link between relative power and pattern of warfighting, embedded in offensive realism. Thus, Israel's example presents a model of the nuclear weaponization effect that does not encourage aggression but also does not impose restraint on the conventional battlefield.

In conclusion, this book could be regarded as a further contribution to the research of nuclear proliferation. By focusing on the analysis of the nuclear weaponization impact on the warfighting patterns in conventional conflicts of the three case studies, it presented a new perspective on the role of nuclear weapons in relations between countries, beyond the discussion mainly devoted to the nuclear weapons contribution to the strategic stability. We hereby provided insights into the way countries form their perception of strategic threats, how they choose patterns of warfighting and most importantly how nuclear weaponization could influence the strategic threat perceptions of decision-makers and consequently a preference of warfighting pattern.

It should be noted that the models of nuclear weaponization impact developed and introduced in this book are not exhaustive. In some countries, decision-makers may perceive nuclear weaponization in a different manner, which does not match the characteristics of any model generated in this research. In this sense, the findings of the research and the theoretical framework applied therein may serve as a basis for conducting further research on the topic. Moreover, the study presents an opportunity for researchers to conduct similar comparative and comprehensive analyses of other case studies that will address the effect of nuclear weaponization on additional parameters, such as the relationship between a nuclear dimension and country's behavior in course of military crisis, which didn't escalate to full-scale conventional wars. These issues are becoming even more relevant and important nowadays as more countries around the world, such as Iran, try to challenge a nuclear weapons proliferation regime and seek to develop their own nuclear arsenal. Further studies can deepen our understanding of the impact of covert nuclear arsenal on countries' conduct in crises and wars. Ultimately, understanding how countries operate and fight under the "undeclared" nuclear umbrella can be helpful in crises and prevent dangerous escalations.

REFERENCES

Khan, F. H. (Spring 2003). Challenges to Nuclear Stability in South Asia. *The Nonproliferation Review*, 59–74.

Mearsheimer, J. (2014). *The Tragedy of Great Power Politics*. New York and London: W. W. Norton.

Narang, V. (2014). *Nuclear Strategy in the Modern Area*. Princeton: Princeton University Press.

Pakistan Should Protect Its National Interest Over Middle East Crisis. (2020, January 7). DAWN. https://www.dawn.com/news/1526716/pakistan-should-protect-its-national-interest-over-middle-east-crisis. Accessed 8 January 2020.

Shilo, T. (2019, November 11). Netanyahu on the Peace with Jordan: "It Is Important to Prevent the Takeover of Islamist Elements". *Walla News*. https://news.walla.co.il/item/3322959. Accessed 9 December 2019 [in Hebrew].

INDEX

© The Editor(s) (if applicable) and The Author(s), under exclusive   163
license to Springer Nature Switzerland AG, part of Springer Nature 2020
I. Davidzon, *Patterns of Conventional
Warfighting under the Nuclear Umbrella*,
https://doi.org/10.1007/978-3-030-45594-1